RECOVERY

DESPITE

REHAB

RECOVERY BEYOND
TWELVE STEP PROGRAMS

SKYLER PENNINGTON

BALBOA.PRESS

A DIVISION OF HAY HOUSE

Balboa Press books may be ordered through booksellers or by contacting:

Balboa Press
A Division of Hay House
1663 Liberty Drive
Bloomington, IN 47403
www.balboapress.com
844-682-1282

ISBN: 978-1-9822-7729-1 (sc)
ISBN: 978-1-9822-7728-4 (e)

Print information available on the last page.

Balboa Press rev. date: 06/10/2022

Shout Outs

To my wonderful family, without whom I never would have survived long enough to write this book! To my mother for her empathy, intelligence, patience, and unconditional love. To my father for his discipline, even-temperedness, unconditional love, and courage.

To my, God rest her soul, aunt and her daughter, the most loving human beings that have ever lived. They can warm the coldest, hardened heart that is accustomed to gritty darkness and teach it the ways of light.

To my childhood friends in Atlanta, I wish nothing but blessings upon you and happiness for all your days and nights.

To my middle school principal, J. C. R., the wisest woman I have ever had the privilege to know.

CONTENTS

CHAPTER 1
RECOVERY DESPITE AUTISM

I WAS BORN ON MARCH 10, 1990. THE DOCTORS TOLD MY PARENTS that I would not survive the night. I was born two months premature, and my stomach and lungs did not function properly. My parents refused to give up this fight despite the doctor's grim prognosis and tended to my need's night and day. I received breast milk through a nasal tube for the first three weeks of life to ensure I received nutrients by the age of 13 months. To the doctors' amazement, I survived. However, this was not the end of my health issues. By thirteen months, the doctors told my family that I had irreversible autism. They told my family I would never speak or develop any relationships. My diagnosis confirmed severe mental retardation. The doctors predicted my future would be one of institutionalization and drugs for me to learn or function at a minimum level. Even in this tragic moment, my family persisted and created a home intervention program based on my developmental needs, with a wonderful team of volunteers! I exhibited outward behaviors to regulate my constant anxiety spikes by walking in circles compulsively. It felt like the world was an intensely tough place for me because I could not take in any sensory information. I walked in circles, wringing my hands together in a squeezing motion, and daydreamed frequently at colors. While it seemed impossible for me to communicate with anyone, I preferred the fantasy world in my head to that of human interaction.

My family and our volunteer team constructed a sensory-calm playroom and played with me twelve hours a day for over four and a half years. Slowly, through all the love, compassion, and attention they offered, I healed in all areas of development—spreading like a ripple throughout my waking hours. But some skeletons had already begun gathering in my closet as this process unfolded.

I have powerful memories dating back to the first time I witnessed people under the influence; that danced, spinning in chairs from my earliest recollections at four years old. I thoroughly enjoyed anything and everything that took me out of reality. Yet today, I have no choice but to face my tendencies towards escapism head-on and to slay my Goliath-sized rock star demons from a sober perspective.

For most people, sobriety is the norm, and we see drug misuse as a dangerous risk. For a drug addict, the risk is sobriety itself and drugs are the comfort zone. Even at this early age, my drug of choice was always *more*. Today, my drug of choice in happy abstinence is STILL, always *more*. It is just that I shifted my craving for the *more*, inevitably, after recovery from a self-destructive way of life and addiction toward experiences that substantiate personal development. I discovered that it is not addiction itself that is evil, but which addictions you chose that determines your life's outcome. Without an obsessive, addictive drive, all the greatest inventions of our time would never exist. Haven't all great artists needed the same addictive drive to make a sociological-cultural impact? To become great requires the same mindset that an addict experiences when their blood boils for the next hotshot, willing to kill or steal to get it. This kind of obsessive mentality, when translated into constructive activities, creates an unstoppable force that can change the world!

By the time I was nine years old, no symptoms of my autistic diagnosis remained, but reality had become an uncomfortable cycle of personal inadequacy and a growing craving for escape. I practiced altering my reality and keeping myself safe. I had little to no fear of altering my consciousness, as I had used behaviors that allowed me to escape my reality from an early age. I knew of my tendencies towards excess in my personality right from the very beginning. Ironically, the same obsessive, detail-oriented and passionate instinct allowed me to graduate college with honors, making the Dean's list five consecutive times and graduating in the top one percent of my entire university. But that same instinct nearly led me to self-destruction as a rail-thin junkie, habituated to nearly every narcotic on the planet with at one point, a serious death wish.

It was that same obsessive mentality that led me beyond just smoking weed. Until I was 29, I made smoking weed my entire identity! This decision turned me away from many opportunities I could have easily experienced given my academic performance. I cared more about getting high and staying high at all costs to self-medicate myself from years of unresolved traumas. These childhood traumas took shape in multifaceted abuse in middle school. Rubber bands shot into my eyes and metal chairs slammed into my skull. Then the trauma was reinforced by my being socially ostracized in high school. I was singled out as a bookworm and a nerd, a status I hold with pride today instead of shame because at that time shame overtook my intelligence and may have been part of why I began misusing drugs; to nullify myself to other people's level. Today I am both clean and damn proud of my nerdy propensities and can say unequivocally to that line of diseased thinking—screw that dogshit mentality! America already embraces enough stupidity we need more nerds, not less.

———●———

Throughout my life, my heroes were musicians and artists. Rebels and the troublemakers. Hardened battle-scarred round pegs in the square holes. Ones who were never fond of the rules. Eccentric individuals who had zero respect for the status quo. This view holds true for me even to this very day, living a far healthier and sober lifestyle. What has changed is my beliefs about non-conformity, embracing a non-destructive way to chase those impulses and channel this energy into creativity, instead of disassociation from reality.

Yet I felt as if I was a born rebel and non-conformist! Destined to color outside society's standards and this still holds true today. My bullying incidents stretched back to the 4th grade, where the rich Jewish kids frequently gave me wedgies and mocked my *full moon* or lack of underwear after the wedgies when I would change pants to prevent said wedgies.

Moving away from my hometown had a profoundly negative impact on my self-esteem, as I had left behind all my close friends and confronted by a hostile social environment where privilege, entitlement, and social status, had higher cultural value than substance or authenticity. My growing social alienation and the resulting traumas that led to my addiction continued from middle school all the way through my first year of college until I was ready to become anesthetized and sedated as a readily available coping mechanism. It is a genuine miracle that I survived and got myself out, as all traditional treatments had made my addiction exponentially worse. There is an implicit reason there is no six-figure income or incentive for the addiction counselors to remain honest with vulnerable & mentally ill people. Better to lie to them and have constantly relapsing, suffering individuals forking out cash into these facilities than teach self-empowerment to anybody, as that would lead to the loss of their entire industrial model.

The actual world had nothing to offer me, anyway. Reality only represented misery, boredom, and superficiality in my mind. Tune in, turn on, and drop out became my religion! I would eventually learn that the short life of excess offers the same emptiness tied beneath a far more seductive yet deceptive package. I went home, locked myself in my room, and repeated the insanity mantra in a mischievous whisper to myself. "When I grow up, I will drink alcohol every day, take all the drugs I want constantly, and get to feel the sensation of happiness, even if it's fake. Better synthetic happiness than no happiness at all." became my motto for life from nineteen to thirty years old. I loved the smell of cases of alcohol. I always associated that smell of liquor with being a sophisticated grownup. I imagined myself being the star of all those seductive misleading alcohol commercials, which projected euphoric fantasies upon my nerdy social outcast mind. I could fantasize about being surrounded by women in scantily clad tight suits with kegs of beer on tap—anything to escape from the periodic trauma filled with life-scaring bouts of bullying and beatings during middle school. Violent incidents left me with full-blown PTSD for over twelve years. I never told my loving family about these incidents because I internalized them to represent my failure as a human being and as a man. This attitude planted the seeds of avoiding any pain and chasing pleasure hedonistically well before taking my first drug or drink. I believed that all pain was only evil, and all pleasure was only beneficial. I blame this perspective for my burgeoning drug addiction, 100x more than any drugs I used or abused. I abused food and video games as my first form of OxyCodone, codeine, nicotine and marijuana (my drugs of choice). I was compulsively playing video games or gorging on food for hours to anesthetize my feelings, problems, and loneliness. When ice cream, tiramisu, and Super Mario stopped giving me the same rush of pleasure and security, I graduated to smoking joints, guzzling liquor, and downing hard narcotics; a deadlier but far more effective set of painkillers.

CHAPTER 2

MY NEED FOR ESCAPE BEGINS

AFTER MIDDLE SCHOOL, I BEGAN ABUSING FOOD AND VIDEO GAMES, not for fun or nutrition, but to deaden my emotions and avoid pain. In doing so without realizing it, I slowly but surely began handicapping my potential as a writer and as a creative artist! Because what is a magnificent work of art if it cannot tap into pain and joy? Life is not happy, nor does life feel good all the time. The natural order of existence is a constant balance. To handle any pleasure, you must experience an equal amount of pain to get that pleasure and happiness. Without pain or boredom, we have no motive for human beings to improve ourselves. The fatal flaw of the drug abusing mindset is the dominant desire to escape all pain and suffering, living vicariously through pleasure to deal with life's harsh edges by blunting them. By numbing that pain, you never learn to adapt or grow from it. Instead, you subconsciously condition yourself to run from pain, just as I escaped through self-medicating with alcohol or drugs in the past. Ironically, I have found purpose and an outlet for my rebellious nature in leading a clean lifestyle because it shows me that anything is possible when you can overcome an addiction that made most rehabs refuse to work with me. After all, I was honestly trying to die so badly. I was not just a drug addict; I had a pathological 25-year-old John Frusciante death wish (Wilonsky, 1–4). Even by the standards of drug addicts, my spiritual energies were black and entangled in the desire to die young because I felt like the entire world was irredeemably evil and the lifestyle of utter darkness and addictions became both an excuse and a coping mechanism. I found addiction was my perfect balance between life and death. Suicide by direct means was unforgivable, but my addiction was a survival technique—a self-destructive tool.

Because I was where you are, and I was far more gone than you or anyone might imagine. I did not know of any such thing as a top to bottom. Rock-bottom. I was twenty thousand feet below the lowest rock bottoms imaginable. That was where my addictions to alcohol, Cannabis, painkillers, and opiates eventually took me. Without psychedelics, my self-destructive ego would have insured my ultimate destruction. Without the revelation's psychedelics forced me to see within myself, I would never have become clean. I would have overdosed and died a miserable sordid death. I could level out and abstain from marijuana and all other drugs for good once my root childhood trauma became uprooted.

Although I would never recommend that anyone do this, magic mushrooms also made it impossible for me to enjoy smoking Cannabis in the same manner forever afterward. I knew Cannabis had become an addiction; it was not something casual for me as with others. It was self-medication, an eventual escape from my responsibilities and my life. I confronted years of demons in powerful waves of hallucinations while listening to psychedelic rock music designed to induce trance states. I experienced the unity of mind, a body of other-worldly authority. It was God reaching directly into my soul and yanking out all the poison and garbage that had accumulated through years of trauma all at once. During the trip, I attempted to smoke a joint, and for the first time in my life, it felt unnatural, like I was smoking a regular cigarette. It felt unhealthy and self-defeating, and ever since Psilocybin, I cannot smoke marijuana without feeling shame, paranoia, or realizing how it both aids and holds me back.

Set refers to your mindset when you engage in any behavior. The *setting* is the people you are with and the environment you interact with during the experience. With a proper set and setting, all human experiences both good and evil, can create profound and long-lasting positive life transformations used with correct intentions and spiritual principles. Do not cling in fondness and weakness to your old ego, for proper intentions with human experiences affords you losing the ability to keep your ego present. When in doubt, trust your companions, relax, and float upstream! On the opposite right end of the spectrum, divorced from either good intentions or spiritual principles involved my eight disastrous years of chronic suicidal alcoholism, a ten-month binge of K2 Spice, and thank God, one ugly single, trial run of methamphetamines (from which I am over nine years clean). Valium, dextromethorphan, and an intense eight-and-a-half-month foray into opiates such as Codeine and my favorite poison of all, 80 mg OxyContin, promptly tore me to pieces and allowed me to hide from myself until I reached absolute rock bottom. I favored the numbing chemical agents for years until I could hide from myself no longer. I was unquestionably the black sheep of the family.

I genetically have little natural ability to use drugs moderately, temperately, or responsibly as others can because of my predisposition towards addictive excess. I can honestly enjoy the effects of psychoactive chemicals, even when I am watching myself destroy and dismantle my life from the inside out! Self-actualized people put their goals before their behaviors, and fragmented people do the exact opposite. Most drugs allow you to escape yourself;

psychedelics directly force users to confront themselves and the truth about their lifestyle. While I would never recommend this method, psychedelics are the only psychoactive I found beneficial because they forced self-actualization and reflection in my experience and forced me to embrace a change of heart and mindset. Magic mushrooms made me realize my real addiction to marijuana and alcohol and how these substances held me back in so many ways in life. Cannabis and alcohol are fine for most people in moderation, but for me, they consumed my entire life and spirit. My life only got better once I quit them for good, God-willing never to return. Cannabis is a drug that, while beneficial for most people used with proper temperance and responsibility, completely took over and consumed my life. I have zero ability ever to use drugs sensibly or healthily because of my highly addictive personality. It would take me a decade to admit this personality trait within myself, to myself. Therefore, drug abuse had to be withdrawn as an option from my life for good, and while I do not regret my experiences as an addict, I have zero wish ever to return! Psychedelics deliberately require unselfishness to get the most out of the incident, and bad trips swiftly punish people who attempt to use them as recreational drugs. They are the only class of psychoactive that not only have I experienced zero addiction with despite powerful experiences, but they have led me to embrace a sober, drug-free lifestyle. Cannabis can potentiate a journey but often makes a trip too intense for newcomers and leads to a bad experience.

Many consider marijuana to be a psychedelic itself. Still, it is only psychedelic with a low tolerance. Marijuana isn't a tryptamine like LSD, mushrooms, or mescaline, and becomes a depressant with a high tolerance in my experience. It is also easy to abuse because overdose is impossible. This description does not stand as a promotion or condone taking anything, as I passionately believe after years of excessive drugging that a clean, sober mind is the most productive and by FAR most prepared mindset to deal with a deadly and unmerciful modern society. Four consecutive failed rehabs, alongside four consecutive failed sober livings, was my resume. A dead man walking, who did not care whether I lived or died. I roamed the streets homeless and strung out on K2 Spice and alcohol, the embodiment of the living dead. I was dragged into poorly managed treatment centers where they dosed me with so much Valium and Thorazine that I became hopelessly addicted to the drugs they gave me to get off alcohol, only to relapse on suicidal drinking after kicking those.

Chronic relapse was my middle name. I cannot even describe to ordinary people how dirty, despicable, and disgusting sobriety feels to an addict who is not ready to stop drinking and using! You feel like your skin is being stripped away like your spirit is getting suffocated by the wreckage of your unresolved traumas, and the only thing you can think of to make it stop is to get as high as possible, as often as possible. I understand why a good deal of hate is dumped on addicts (drugs are unnecessary to become an addict). We will feed our addictions over prioritizing you every single time once a craving gets powerful enough. We will lie, cheat, steal and do whatever is necessary to get our favorite brand of poison flowing through us. It need not be drugs at all. Any behavior that brings pleasure can become a destructive coping mechanism, even healthy outlets when taken too far because your idea of poison is our idea of medicine to soothe the soul and awaken the senses. The biggest flaw of the modern rehabilitation system in America is that they treat drug abuse as the **ONLY** problem. It is nearly symptomatic of a much deeper issue, and addiction does not discriminate between drugs or anything else. Authorities design our corrupt system to perpetuate a vicious cycle of revolving-door patients consistently.

The tough love and one-size-fits-all policy denies the underlying pain that drove everyone into mental-illness or a destructive lifestyle of self-medicating. While this is failure for the afflicted, the practitioners make six figures annually from this evil, and they have no desire to change this broken system. We must force them to change this system, or thousands more will die from both untreated mental illness & untreated addiction. The pain and loneliness of addiction know no cultural or socioeconomic boundaries. The opposite of addiction is not sobriety. It is a connection, a connection to a higher purpose, a connection to people who love you unconditionally and see you as more outstanding than you can see yourself.

After middle school, I was never the same. PTSD that had been dormant until then exposed itself to the ugly surface. By high school, constant PTSD flashbacks impaired my daily functioning at intolerable levels, which burdened nearly every activity. Where I did not know when I was in the past or the present and did not care. Metal chairs flew into my face randomly. Randomly; rubber bands materialized out of thin air, snapping to my eyelids. Hallucinogenic blood splatters would temporarily blind me every few minutes. I would hallucinate cascading pools of blood that were never there. Even worse was the fact that I sadly believed that all these episodes were entirely my fault alone. I deserved to get beaten up and ostracized by everyone else. My self, as my authentic self, was unworthy of love or life.

My PTSD and the self-doubts that these events fueled within my raging subconscious became so unbearable, I did not tell my loving family and withdrew deep into my psyche and became sicker and sicker by the day, until darkness consumed my soul for years. The world daily feels like an empty black abyss when you experience depression—a useless gray pool of shadowy, meaningless anti-matter. Without my knowledge, I became surrounded by dark, evil spirits that sought to influence my behavior. These spirits only allowed me to see everything in life that pulled me towards the welcoming hand of death. I did not realize that I was suffering from severe depression and PTSD. These PTSD episodes only grew in intensity and made social interaction progressively more and more unbearable while sober. I set up a pattern of escapism, self-medicating daily with anything I could find (not just drugs and alcohol) that would last many years until I cultivated a necessary lifestyle of self-discipline while keeping faithful to a proud existence of nonconformity. It is easy to follow the herd and do what everyone else does, sober or not, but it takes true courage and strength to go against the grain, against the dissenters, to forge your truth.

I had used no alcohol or drugs in high school until I was 19 and started drinking to get drunk habitually. I stole a bottle of wine during Passover and chugged half the bottle in under five minutes. I became a sloppy drunk from day one and eventually graduated into the violent, belligerent drunk alcoholic with ease. Wasn't the fun frat party drunk? As on the run for your mother-fucking life, someone's property, shoulders, or intestines are getting dislocated drunk from day one. My life was transformed forever into the passionate, psychotic pursuit of intoxication! Now I realized I could take chemicals that instantly changed how I felt from depression to expression, and the dice rolled for the next nine years—I got supremely wasted beyond conception! I never cared to drink socially, only binge gulping. My preferred method from the start was utter oblivion by strict dietary preferences. Clumsily bumping into furniture and spilling every glass I touched while vomiting my guts out in the bathroom.

A tattered canvas of shredded matzah, mixed delicately with the subtle aroma of upchucked wine, floating in leftover Matzo Ball Soup. I had to flush three times to remove the damage. I even made a pass at a random girl before spending the first night of much more to come puking my innards out. I never bought into the disease model of addiction for a simple reason. I always, 1000% of the time, chose to drink and use drugs and was always fully conscious of my reasons for drinking and using. Even when the basis for using substances were self-destructive or non-consciousness expanding, addiction was always a choice. I rooted my habits in simultaneous escapism from underlying severe trauma, many wounds, and scars, of which I am still healing from today. It is not drug use that causes the evils of addiction but the mindset you adopt when going into the experience that determines the outcome.

My philosophy was that I did not like or accept pain, so why not consistently alter its structure to my exact liking? This mentality and the ensuing behaviors which followed that destructive mindset, not the drugs, was my primary downfall. My father had to drag me out of the bathroom as I vomited everywhere. I continued to vomit all the way home in a car ride so disturbingly silent, a pin could drop, and a New Zealander could hear it from California. Regardless of the embarrassment I may have caused, all I remembered was that I felt comfortably numb, happy, and unconcerned with any of my problems. Nor was I remotely bothered by my flagrant neuroticism. Nor bothered by increased pathological and antisocial tendencies whenever I became drunk, and especially when I got high.

My attraction to getting high began well before I smoked my first marijuana cigarette. By nineteen, I was popping prescription painkillers and benzodiazepines, such as Vicodin and Valium. Drugs like this were my gateway to a 100 gram per day opiate addiction to OxyContin and codeine because I finally felt comfortable in my skin for the first time. I knew from the moment I altered my consciousness that I would do just about anything and everything under the sun not to have to face reality and that I was addicted—although I did not admit it to myself at first. I did not like myself in high school, so I became a practicing drug addict by senior year because, at the time, it gave me a sense of rebellious identity, which I was honestly proud of for many years.

During the height of my addiction, I did not care about the consequences because the drugs allowed me to hide from myself and my insecurities so effectively. I became utterly convinced I would never be sober as soon as I began experimenting with drugs because they took all my pain and insecurities away in the beginning, just like magic! I was already off the rails using hard drugs well before I experimented with Cannabis and hallucinogens. Today my pride comes from dropping using drugs as a lifestyle, never to return God willing to the minefield of daily substance abuse. Any mind-altering experiences (particularly those that are chemical) that people engage in without the goal of spiritual transcendence, fun, or consciousness expansion, have the inevitable intent of escapism rooted in self-delusion and denial leading inevitably to self-destruction and utter ruin.

CHAPTER 3

MY LOVE OF DRUGS & ALCOHOL BEGINS

AFTER EIGHT TERRIBLE YEARS OF ESCALATING DEPRESSION AND prolonged isolation following violent, intensifying bullying incidents in middle school, all primed me to become a substance abuser by my senior year. When I began using drugs and alcohol, it felt as if a switch flipped on. It was indeed a divine miracle at first! Those persistent feelings of seething self-hatred and despair suddenly did not influence my happiness at all when I became stoned (or so I believed at first). I suddenly felt just like everyone else in the world, no better or worse than anyone else! I had just as much and was as big as the next person, no matter what I accomplished in this life or not. I fell hopelessly in love with alcohol and drugs at that very moment. It would take a decade before the wool and fog lifted, and I realized what my dependency and lack of temperance had stolen from me.

Getting high was utterly remarkable and enjoyable for the first two years. This was the golden age before my entire world came crashing down! I experienced a watershed moment in my existence where a wholly unfamiliar world opened. A world filled with light and wonder, where before, there was a sea of absolute darkness and self-hatred. I believed for a genuine moment that I had slipped into a new skin. An identity with self-confidence instead of endless fear or frailty; defined by humor and synthetic peace instead of melancholy and depression! I was a man who took pleasure in others' company and felt equal to others, instead of reveling in isolation with worries of inferiority and obsessive self-loathing.

I did not take drugs to feel superior to anyone else, nor did I feel superior to anyone under the influence. My attraction to drugs was feeling exactly like everyone else, no more significant than or less than equal. I did not care about the cost of my drug habit; I felt zero shame or dread about the trials to follow when I willingly graduated from being a recreational drug user from nineteen to twenty to a full-blown addict at twenty-one. I would chase that feeling of artificial synthetic happiness to the very ends of the Earth, even if it killed me! Because I was already dead and beaten-up inside with years of unresolved PTSD and the mental scars that followed, despite attempts at therapy that went poorly. So why not stay wasted, stoned, tripping & high until I died? When one of my relatives realized I was severely struggling with my demons and going down fast, he reached out to me, crying. He became terrified that I would go down the same path as he had experimented with, having abused drugs himself in the sixties. He was very wrong. I was a million times worse than he had ever been with an incomprehensible Kurt Cobain level drug habit (Romance, 1).

Contrary to this relative's experiences, I did not have a drug of choice. I liked anything and everything that altered my consciousness, no matter the consequences, for a solid decade. He warned me that I was heading down a black path from which I might never fully recover from. I remained too lost and selfish to comprehend his love or his warnings while white-knuckling short and agonizing dry periods were ravenously cleaning out my parent's liquor cabinet. Preoccupied, I would constantly spend my days smoking too much weed by the ounce and gobbling down hard narcotics with an unquenchable, rock star appetite. I could not comprehend what he was telling me through the haze because the haze was more important to me than my happiness. The weed smoke was more important to me than my own life or well-being because I did not care about myself enough.

Multi-day hangovers from alcohol and benzos made me desperate for anything that would numb the pain of increasing withdrawal symptoms and my growing abyss of self-loathing. I experimented with harder narcotics consistently when I was wasted on liquor. As these withdrawal symptoms intensified, so did my abuse of Valium and other prescription painkillers. I could quickly get whatever I needed at any school parking lot or the medicine cabinets of friends and family. Initially, for my first two years of smoking weed (the same years that I used drugs only on weekends before I became an addict), my use was all about consciousness expansion through the psychoactive effects that drastically improved my creativity and drive initially. Had I been able to use the drugs temperately, I might have had zero issues. But the desire for the euphoric escape drugs provided for me, even when my tolerance was high enough that all the positive effects vanished, crowded out everyone and everything else that was important to my life.

After my first two years experimenting with drugs, I made a very conscious decision to be under the influence of drugs all the time. Never guilty was I of my choices. I was always proud of being a drug addict, a vanguard of the counterculture. I was proud of going against the grain of what society's expectations were of people, rebelling, and I instantly identified with the outcasts, mentally ill, and rejected people whom society deemed as worthless. I also felt like I needed to be a drug addict to cope with a modern society I found repetitive and unbearably cruel. I cannot describe in words how disgusting and utterly horrible sobriety feels to an addict who is not ready to stop drinking and using (not referring to recreational users or normies). You feel unclean every sober moment, like your numb to happiness. You care far too much what everyone thinks about you, and you are in a constant state of self-loathing and shame because you see how your addiction has destroyed your lifestyle in those brief moments of clarity. Then the craving for drugs becomes the fix for the addiction itself. By the end of my drug addiction and my addiction to mind-altering substances, I used drugs to mitigate the consequences that directly resulted from my drug misuse.

After my first two years of smoking weed and experimenting with drugs recreationally, I decided I loved drugs so much that I would not skip a day of using and would stay under the influence as if habitual intoxication was a sign of devout religious piety. I began smoking weed and taking drugs routinely every single day and night. Then the dice immediately rolled for me over the next eight years, and I went off the rails, becoming frozen in time. As I graduated into a practicing pothead and eventual full-blown junkie, my natural innate creativity and ambitions slowly devolved into my being solely focused on abusing the drugs and smoking weed to feel *right* without my recognizing this change at all. Unlike recreational users, to a drug addict, the norm is being loaded. Sobriety in the counterculture is out of fashion and hurts far too much. I thought the drugs went along with my creative ambitions, spiritual philosophies, and goals as they had at first. I believed drugs would profoundly enhance my lifestyle, social connections, and long-term goals my first two years—my only two years of moderate intake. But getting high became the goal itself and supplanted all my genuine passions and dreams. My lifestyle became very dark, and I was constantly subject to infiltration from evil and destructive spirits. That is when you have crossed an uncrossable line from a recreational drug user into a drug addict. That line is impossible to uncross once you step over it without constant self-deception and inevitable self-destruction.

Psychedelics such as salvia, LSD, 4-ACO DMT, and magic mushrooms have always had the opposite effect on my psyche. These substances always forced me to look at myself—who I was as an addict. There was a duality within me that questioned who I wanted to become as a person while avoiding personal issues by stuffing down my pain through excessive self-abuse. I do not condone the use of psychoactive substances for anyone. Still, I would argue that having a clear, sober mind to face your problems is always 100% better than hiding or masking your troubles away with abusing drugs or dopamine-releasing behaviors, an eventual self-destructive coping mechanism. Based on Leary's experiences (1966), psychedelics are the opposite of drugs you used to escape from reality, in that the psychedelic experience makes you directly confront yourself and your perceptions of reality. You cannot take them on a whim. If your mindset is not healthy or positive, or you are not living a balanced, healthy lifestyle and fully pursuing your ambitions and goals, tryptamines will crush your ego like a grape. They will make you wish you could visit Hell as a vacation from the experience they will force upon you if not treated with the utmost respect and caution. Uniquely, it is because of tryptamine psychedelics I remain Alcohol, Cannabis & opiate-free to this very day when all other treatments had done little or nothing to get me to stop my destructive alcoholism. Perhaps Cannabis is a psychedelic itself, but because you can take it for euphoria regardless of your mental state, I would argue that it is not in the same class despite its psychedelic tryptamine effects as a mild hallucinogen. After only one experience with magic mushrooms, I finally kicked marijuana and other drugs for good. It showed me how drugs had officially stopped serving me. I slowly realized that I continued in my delusion when I used drugs to excess without temperance or personal responsibility. Yet, thinking I would get anywhere I wanted to in life habitually intoxicated would ensure that I would pay a hefty and well-deserved price for my denial. After this experience, I have happily pledged a lifestyle of total abstinence to extreme temperance in my drug consumption for the rest of my life. My religious fascination and addictive obsession with drugs stole most of my twenties away from me. I had lost years, and I never want to waste one more precious second of the life I have remaining!

In my experience, Cannabis was the only hallucinogen I became emotionally addicted to using. Only opiates and Cannabis consistently gave me this powerful feeling. "Aaaaahhh… my life is complete, and I don't feel a hopeless hole inside the depths of my soul. This high is how I always want to feel and who I want to be for the rest of my life." feeling that pot and opiates have always given me, from the moment I started until the very moment I quit. From the very beginning, until the moment I stopped abusing the drug, only opiates & Cannabis gave me that feeling of completion. The emotional holes disappearing, feeling comfortable and okay inside my skin for the first time in my life. Few other drugs ever gave me that sense of completion inside. That is why I know I will always remain psychologically dependent on marijuana. I pray that I never use it again because Cannabis stole my entire twenties away from me and did more damage to my psyche and life goals than all the other drugs combined. Pot is also the only drug where I lived in continuous, unflagging denial of my psychological addiction to the high. With alcohol, psychedelics, and even many hard drugs, I was always conscientious. I always stopped myself if I felt like I was going over a dangerous limit, consistently overestimating the danger levels. Despite my experiences as an alcoholic who once even drank myself into life-threatening delirium tremens, I never obsessed about alcohol except for filling social phobias. After delirium, I always would drink carefully and suddenly stop myself if I saw myself becoming even mildly drunk. However, I have since learned casual drinking for me, turns into binge drinking really fast. Terrified of going down the black rabbit hole of alcoholism once more, I have since quit.

I have **NEVER** set similar limits with marijuana, constantly underestimating its potency and the spirit dampening powers of habitual long-term smoking and making it the most dangerous drug for me bar none. Because I conditioned my mind to believe pot is innocuous and harmless to use habitually, I could not set limits effectively with pot as with other narcotics. Even today, Cannabis is the only drug that I could so easily lie to myself about and quickly see myself sliding back into semi-daily to daily abuse from that at-first innocuous deceptive occasional toke. Weed is the one substance that deceives me most. The one drug I will use in the most addictive patterns. I denied steadfastly that there was even a problem because of Cannabis use. I made complacency and rationalizations the most dangerous weapons against my recovery. Pot and opiates are the only drugs I have taken that I could feel comfortable lying to myself and deceiving myself about my level of usage. No matter how long I stay sober, no matter how many changes I make, this is my one crucial weakness as this will never change, even if I never touch Cannabis or opiates again.

When I am high, I am ultimately no longer the usual, empathetic, loving person anymore, whether I care to admit this or not, because all I can care about is drugs. If I stay clean for 50 years and smoke even one joint, nothing about this will change. I intend to live out the rest of my life with the utmost temperance and self-restraint. Most all addicts have a love–hate relationship with their addiction of choice. I only changed my habits because I saw what *love* and obsession eventually took away. These damaged my life after a prolonged decade of denial about the consequences of my addiction. By the end of 2019, I was nearly broke and isolated from everyone and everybody and became so strung out that, sadly, I did not see the problem until I stepped out of the haze. Not worth it in the long run! I will never know whether I would have had issues or not had I practiced temperance.

My experience demonstrated that moderation is almost an impossibility for me because abusing drugs and alcohol tore my life apart. I had willingly slid into complacency, stagnation, and eventually mediocrity; I still loved the drugs' effects far too much to imagine quitting—a true addict's hallmark. I also realized that what drug abuse gave me was a few hours of intense euphoria and freedom from boredom and loneliness. The last two perceived benefits were why I stayed true to my addictions, even when I knew it was both killing me and not as intense or fulfilling as in the beginning. The asking price of chemical euphoria over the last two years was the destruction of everything else I cared about in my life and flushing my relationships with the people I love and care about straight down the drain. No euphoria in the world can shield the sadness and darkness of that realization away.

Love is the most dangerous emotion in the world, not hate or even fear. Love can blind human beings to morality, reason, or common sense when it is robust enough. Between Orwell's (1949) assertion that the thing's humanity fears will destroy us and Huxley's (1932) stance that the thing's humanity loves will destroy us, I side 10,000% with Huxley to the very end. What we love can blind us to reason. It can blind us to self-worth, can blind us to personal development, and can even supplant our morality and ethics when we love something enough that we will make irrational and destructive sacrifices to maintain that love. The most critical lesson that poly-drug addiction taught me that love could be beautiful. Still, it can also become deadlier than a cobra's venom and destroy your entire sense of self, your goals, and your self-respect without self-control.

I wish the value of self-control and choosing your obsessions with great care and discipline was a required class for every child. Frankly, such a class needs to become required by international law, as it would provide more value to society than math, English, or science. It did not matter that I was a straight-A student; I was always a highly impulsive, risk-taking individual with little self-control for either my virtues or vices and I knew it well before I touched any drugs.

Temperance / moderation with drugs for me is essential but next to impossible. I am all or nothing with drugs and, in the end, always will be. The moment I forget this, I am doomed and will have to throw it all away for good. People who use drugs in moderation have one trait—discipline—that I will likely never have, no matter how long I am sober, and I do not care anymore. They do not think about using in between using. It is not a lifestyle for them. The decision to take it or leave it is automatic. This is because their goals matter more to them than their behaviors matter. I crossed that invisible line after my first two years of using and have never gotten it back since. I obsessed over learning how to moderate my drug use, so I did not have to quit, whereas people who successfully moderate do not care. They do not crave it. It is just something they enjoy. I never will moderate drugs long-term, given my track record of attempting temperance with narcotics. People who use drugs in moderation lead balanced lives, in which drugs are not a constant focus. They do not even think about it. Moderation exists for them because it is something they do for fun, not escape or to self-medicate deeper underlying issues.

I discreetly, desperately tried for years to find that balance with my drug intake and never could. My only focus was on the drugs and controlling the uncontrollable for me which I steadfastly denied to my detriment, even when I was not drinking or using. I also rejected that my drug use was more for self-medicating relief from trauma and inner insecurities than for pleasure. After two years, consciousness expansion or fun changed for most of my drug-using career, because drugs spiraled into the sole purpose of self-medication and became my entire way of life. All I wanted to do was to run away and hide from creeping feelings of failure, rejection, and loneliness. What allowed me to quit for good was finally admitting that I seldom enjoyed others company whenever I controlled my drug intake. Whenever I let myself fully indulge, I used to dangerous, often life-threatening excesses! That is a sacrifice I am no longer willing to make. Many addicts obsess over learning to control their drug use. In contrast, people who moderate never think about it. It is a non-issue for them because their life goals matter more, and they can still enjoy recreational drug use without it becoming a lifestyle.

To a drug addict, their life goals become secondary to the high of the drugs and the behaviors surrounding drug misuse. At first, my life goals and creativity were far more critical than drinking or using in my first two years using drugs. Even though I enjoyed smoking weed and getting drunk, I was sober all week and moderated because I wanted to graduate at the top of my class. The next eight years it was a 180° pancake flip for me because I rationalized to myself that drugs made me feel so good and so comfortable in my skin that sobriety became unbearable. This was the moment my life began to self-destruct. Why not be under the influence all the time? With honest self-reflection, those eight years, the highs from the drugs or the behaviors that allowed me to hide from myself eventually supplanted my actual values, goals, and creativity. For the next eight years, I was an addict, and what I cared about was drugs and nothing else. Even worse was that until 2020, I was either unaware of this process or denied it vehemently, and I cannot think of anything more horrible. I also know myself well enough to state that even if I stay clean for decades, if I tempt fate again by relapsing, it will **NEVER** stay recreational for long before the 800-pound gorilla is calling all the shots in my life, not me. I never used drugs after my first year of experimenting just for fun or consciousness expansion. My primary reason for drinking and using was to mask pain, loneliness, and boredom. Therefore, I cannot touch them ever again if I ever expect to fulfill my true creative potential. If I could have been temperate, that would have been fine. Still, after my first two years of psychoactive exploring, I could never moderate intelligently after the only two years I was ever intelligent about the subject of drugs. I kept my intake strictly to Friday's and Saturday's until I decided I wanted to feel that way all the time, and the downward spiral began.

In my opinion, drugs do not ruin your life because they are bad. They consume your energy because they are honestly far too good to be true, and have no right being as amazing as they are! How could drugs ruin people's lives if they were bad or didn't give something to users, no one would want to take them! They make people euphoric and too comfortable with their current reality, eventually stifling self-development and personal growth. When drugs are abused the high becomes the only focus for any self-respecting drug addict. Drugs set a new benchmark for fun. Fill holes inside your spirit and soul that can become profoundly difficult to match when freshly sober, once the user become habituated to pushing chemical pleasure buttons over tolerating sober discomforts that are a part of life, evolution, and personal spiritual growth. Drugs also make it far too easy to forget or bypass morals, goals, and values. Lifestyle's people may have spent an entire lifetime developing become unimportant because users can get short-term instant happiness chemically. Some user's mindset fixates on why not push those buttons all the time, if I can get the result without the work it takes in a sober state to reach the same contentment?

I did just this without forethought after my first year of recreational use and nearly destroyed my life. By the time an addict sees the error in pursuing constant chemical pleasure over reality, it is often too late, and their life has utterly fallen apart, into self-destructive chaos and unmanageability. Some never make it back; others live in denial for years and are miserable and broken on the inside. I fight in recovery living to see America's corrupt and ineffectual mental healthcare system altered. Most rehabilitation clinics and sober livings have a purely destructive revolving door which favors tough love, hot seat approaches. The vultures that profit from it should forever lose their six-figure salaries and all fundamental human rights that they have no problem stripping from both drug addicts, alcoholics, and severely mentally ill people for their financial gain! These profits over people institutions are the unfortunate peanut butter and jelly of American mental healthcare; there is an exceptional place in hell reserved for them.

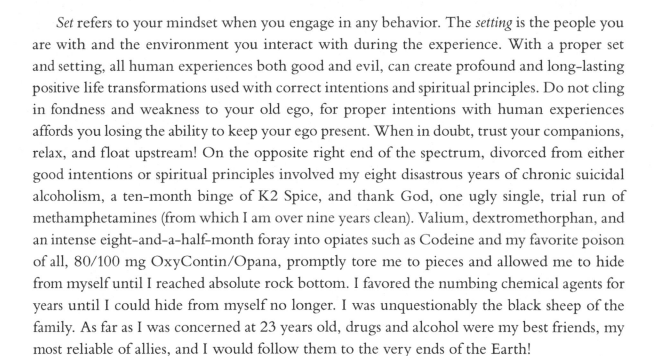

Set refers to your mindset when you engage in any behavior. The *setting* is the people you are with and the environment you interact with during the experience. With a proper set and setting, all human experiences both good and evil, can create profound and long-lasting positive life transformations used with correct intentions and spiritual principles. Do not cling in fondness and weakness to your old ego, for proper intentions with human experiences affords you losing the ability to keep your ego present. When in doubt, trust your companions, relax, and float upstream! On the opposite right end of the spectrum, divorced from either good intentions or spiritual principles involved my eight disastrous years of chronic suicidal alcoholism, a ten-month binge of K2 Spice, and thank God, one ugly single, trial run of methamphetamines (from which I am over nine years clean). Valium, dextromethorphan, and an intense eight-and-a-half-month foray into opiates such as Codeine and my favorite poison of all, 80/100 mg OxyContin/Opana, promptly tore me to pieces and allowed me to hide from myself until I reached absolute rock bottom. I favored the numbing chemical agents for years until I could hide from myself no longer. I was unquestionably the black sheep of the family. As far as I was concerned at 23 years old, drugs and alcohol were my best friends, my most reliable of allies, and I would follow them to the very ends of the Earth!

CHAPTER 4

STRAIGHT-EDGED HEDGE-MAZE EDUCATION

MY EDUCATION ABOUT DRUGS BEGAN IN MIDDLE SCHOOL. OUR CLASS viewed a D.A.R. E *training* session about the temptation of psychoactive chemicals and how they were *bad* without any details or context. Zero harm reduction policies were at all clear. Objective information was not on the cards, and scare tactics were the meal of the day, tactics which were poorly executed which failed at keeping over half the class off drugs and alcohol. A toothless angel dust smoker and crack cocaine addict shuffled in front of dusty chalkboards and impressionable adolescent minds to regale us with tales of sucking dick for his next hit of rock cocaine. It was easy to see that his eyes had thick layers of jaundice, his arms were scarred black and blue from the open lines of seasoned track marks, and the markings of brushing his several missing teeth with bags of P.C.P. and crack. Then the D.A.R. E conglomerate showed the class an enormous image of a pot leaf on a projector. D.A.R.E claimed users would face exponential detriments to their I.Q. from even a single puff of a "gateway marijuana cigarette." This is an ironic statement in my experience for two reasons. I started with alcohol and tobacco, not marijuana, as my gateway drugs to more complex narcotics. And second, I was already off the rails experimenting with opiate derivatives, benzos, and harsh synthetics at nineteen, well before I even smoked my first joint! It was my dirty little secret that would soon become no secret to anyone who knew me. If America cares about public health, D.A.R. E needs to be banned from all forms of educating children regarding drugs and alcohol.

The "Just Say No" approach has never worked; we need to include harm reduction in every classroom for the people who do eventually partake to keep them safe and avoid addiction.

The value of self-discipline and self-control, time management, let alone money management skills were not taught to me during my formal education or at home, to my serious detriment in my twenties. These skills must become required learning for every child if we expect a solid and healthy society, or we are flushing our children's potential down the sewer in favor of lies and scare tactics. Using lies to keep people away from dangerous activities encourages reverse psychology; this only makes people desire the *Forbidden Fruit*. In my opinion, legalizing all drugs removes the illicit thrill and desire to rebel that many teenagers use as an excuse to begin experimentation. If drugs were legal and strictly regulated, they would become as boring a topic as possible, eliminating the glamor element. Danger and pain are a part of life. We cannot shield people from themselves or reality. We expect them to develop and adapt towards functioning within the contexts of an increasingly fragmented and complex modern world.

My faithful and close friends visited me a few times in future rehab visits. Still, they soon stopped coming over because they already knew that I was slowly, but surely, killing myself. They had no desire to watch my ugly, downward spiral of perpetual self-destruction. I did not rekindle those relationships with my closest friends until I finally got my head out of the sand and out of my ass. I had to realize that temperance/moderation with drugs for me is nearly impossible! As an addict, I liked the escape drugs provided, ensuring that my addiction took over my life, unlike other recreational drug users who were able to prioritize goals over their behaviors! In recovery, I have the unfortunate ability to realize I enjoy drugs and alcohol long after they have taken over and destroyed my lifestyle. No matter how long I stay clean, that demon is always lurking in the shadows, waiting for the moment I let my guard down. I also know that even if I stay clean for decades, and then engage in occasional use, it will not remain occasional use for long! When' D.A.R. E described the potential of LSD for inducing hallucinations and flashbacks, I already knew, and everyone in the class already well understood, that the pitch had utterly failed the entire class. Several kids were already talking excitedly over prepackaged lunches about a sudden interest in smoking marijuana, getting drunk, taking assortments of drugs, and dropping acid. I deeply wanted to experiment with alcohol and drugs from those pitches. We already well knew that as students we were not receiving any proper education on drugs. The lurid descriptions of their effects made them very tempting. I was particularly interested in how music might sound different or how the activities I usually did would feel under the influence of drugs and alcohol. This was the mindset that I brought into college, and the beginning of my drug experimentation.

As I entered college my experiences with drugs were unforgettable. I remember there was a time where the sky seemed to be a haze of thick luminescent vapors, scintillated through the delicious tangerine fragrance of billowing clouds containing thick and pungent marijuana smoke. I was a deeply traumatized, self-destructive, and rampantly lost sophomore at a southwestern university; this university was not unique and represents the students' experiences at too many American colleges. My experience of flagrant neuroticism, a pantheon of insecurities and crippling self-doubts were ripe to be neutered through gratuitous university exposure to sex, drugs, and alcohol. Testing this theory, I attended two Muse concerts with a sympathetic friend. One show I experienced while sober, yet when the other show followed, I was buzzed on liquor and intoxicated on strong weed. The entire crowd waved up and down as I hallucinated, seeing the stage in the shape of an accordion. It was the most incredible concert of my whole life! I heard the music as if I were sitting in the front row, though I remained seated in the stadium bleachers. I then somehow drove home 80 miles while drunk and stoned without getting pulled over.

God must have been watching over me that very near-fatal night, as it was one of the rare nights at twenty-one, I did not black out or become comatose drunk. I was broken mentally, spiritually, and eventually physically, already a full-blown alcoholic. Even by their own standards, most alcoholics refused to associate with me because my excessive drinking turned me into the living embodiment of Satan. No other drug in the whole world can turn me into a conscienceless monster like liquor. I started with drinking beer on weekends, as many do. Multiple forty-ounce bottles and cases of beer became as casual to me as a single glass of wine in the evening for a regular person! Then I quickly proceeded to liters of hard liquor and began experimenting with Lucifer's favorite water form, caffeine mixed with 12% alcohol by volume.

In my opinion, it is not the drugs that are evil, or Satan possessed, it is only the behavior of the drug addict who abuses or misuses them. Labeling drugs as the root of addiction is a copout for people's maladaptive behavior. We can engage in maladaptive behaviors, not doing drugs at all. That is why we love scapegoating or crafting illusions about our behavior and our conduct. However, I genuinely believe that K2 spice, opiates, crystal methamphetamines, crack cocaine, and caffeinated alcoholic beverages were created to destroy humanity by the devil himself. Caffeine mixed with 12 ABV gets you not just drunk, more like Phineas Gage (Smithsonian Magazine, 2-3) drunk with hallucinations like Albert Hofmann's bad acid trips from Lucifer's Garden drunk (Gilmore, 3-5). Now my problems truly began with alcohol. Several shots of expresso topped off with the alcoholic equivalent of six shots of vodka skyrocketed my tolerance to where I started getting withdrawal symptoms without drinking that began to slowly, but surely, impair my daily functioning without my awareness while slowly driving me insane. I would label anyone who would pour their vodka or whiskey into a mixed drink with orange juice, cola, or ginger ale, as a total pussy. I preferred drowning myself in liquor straight with no chaser like any professional practicing alcoholic. My favorite form of alcohol in college was the infamous combination of 12% ABV and a ton of caffiene. The best description of this drink is to think of it as a legal version of cocaine, distilled into a drinkable can jam packed with scotch. They combined 12% liters of alcoholic content by volume, with enough caffeine to awaken an ancient sleeping mummy. The average amount warned to consume was never over three drinks. At times, I have told women drink no more than one alcoholic beverage if it has caffeine in it. My intake was at least three and sometimes five high caffeinated alcoholic beverages regularly for about five years, blacking out nearly every time I imbibed. I counteracted the psychotic damage to my liver and brain by smoking enormous amounts of Cannabis 24/7. At first, I would only binge drink at night on beer and vodka. However, after a night of drinking my morning maintenance including beer or several shots became required. I needed to dull my oppressive horror of bone ripping intestinal shakes and my flesh curtailing sweats which soaked my bed in perspiration, in addition to urine, and vomit unless I guzzled down the first shot or red solo cup of beer. In college, surrounded by drugs and constant partying, I believe that my substance abuse was an adaptation to the chaotic, enabling environment around me; my drug use was a way to gain popular favor and acceptance. The only trouble was it was to get approval with a crowd of brilliant but lost souls stuck in the endless desert of university years.

To describe the squalor of hell that is a desert town fraternity college is to represent a bottomless hole of hellish insanity engulfed in quicksand; the devil himself would squirm away in terror to avoid this dead end. Thousands of kids let loose from their parents for the first time, partying and debauchery at the front of their singularly focused minds. An entirely isolated and fragmented community surrounded by vacant, deserted streets caked in stale beer cans and good old-fashioned shantytown apathy. A single supermarket perched in the town square where kids would routinely steal beer by the caseload, getting trashed in the parking lots as they snorted cocaine. They were students trapped in an endless maze of temptation in this college city, where strip clubs appeared to line nearly every highway intersection. Plentiful hard drug dealers were around every corner, with the cheapest and best methamphetamines and heroin available—several on-duty cops were customers themselves. Only a single movie theater existed, complete with blurry Technicolor screens covered in cobwebs and piles of beer cans could be seen littering the floors. The movie theater staffs did not bother cleaning up the mess, as they often drank the mess themselves. It was a bin of sin. Ghost town mom-and-pop stores were decorated with plastic signs, advertising to plastic people, with broken plastic smiles. Billboard signs were perpetually goading me on to invest in consumer treats that would temporarily, yet ultimately, prove futile in masking my treasure chest of self-insecurities.

The desert town seemed overpopulated by bitter alcoholic baby boomers. These were people who lived and breathed in a state of perpetual upper-middle-class apathy and complacency. I constantly saw fat, bulbous, fast-food burger rumps at the gas pumps, who had little care for college kids' disillusionments. They were too busy chain-smoking cigarettes and drinking themselves to death to notice, let alone care, about the drug problems or their blatant hypocrisy. It seemed to be a boundless ocean of Hummer's and gas-gulping S.U.V.s extending for miles across every lane. Some vehicles double-parked on public property without fear of arrest or citation. No one gave two shits about where you parked because the cops were too drunk or obese themselves to bother writing tickets, let alone arrest criminals. The cops seemed to be four-hundred-pound behemoth limp wads of fat, all supremely hungover. They were fueled by eating pounds of donut sugar, while drinking overflowing oceans of alcohol and testosterone pill cocktails which had expired years ago in dusty forlorn cabinets. They would toddle about with the grace of a beached whale, more concerned with getting their daily *fix* of devil donuts and espresso latte shots laced with alcohol to beat back multi-day hangovers, than attending to the excessive amounts of local drug dealing. Constant noise complaints followed them from bleary-eyed, chain-smoking soccer moms. This college scene painted a disturbing picture of shattered glass, drunken hookups, clear flowing rivers of narcotics, and the loud cries of strangulated innocence. Ninety-eight percent of the time, local complaints involved drunken frat students damaging private property and ending up in the drunk tank. An army of college fraternities and sororities strung out on liquor, cocaine, heroin, marijuana, Red Bull, and endless sex. Nearly everyone smoked weed and crack cocaine like packs of cigarettes. College communities like this one have no foundations of culture or hobbies present to stave away the demons of boredom, so disillusioned populations permit and encourage every vice imaginable; nothing was forbidden.

The first time I smoked Cannabis, my life changed forever! Now in recovery, I can say that these changes were 100% positive and negative changes. While the negatives might seem obvious, in retrospect and from a sober perspective now, my creativity and appreciation for music were all greatly improved due to my experiences with marijuana. However, these positives only correlate to what I implement in my sober lifestyle, and I have often fallen for the trap of relapsing on Cannabis to, *chase the magic* of these assets which were only present the first two years of my drug use. In my first experience with an illegal drug (at the time), I honestly believed I had found God. In one blinding flash, I had discovered the entire meaning of life itself! A devout and pathological Cannabis smoker was born until 2020 when I finally gave up Cannabis for good, God willing never to return to the bittersweet arms of mother hemp! While for the first two years I did not regret any of my experiences with Mary Jane or intermittent drugs, the next eight years were anything but blissful. During those two years, I placed in the top 1% of my university and made the Dean's list five consecutive times despite intermittent weekend use. This was more about my work ethic however, than drug induced productivity. Cannabis has permanently enabled me to hear music much more vividly while sober. It felt as if Cannabis enhanced my creativity during my first two years of use. I suppose that the many psychedelic trips and visions I experienced permanently changed how I look at the nature of reality. Cannabis also gave me a genuine empathy with underdogs, outcasts, and societal deviants that most people refuse to acknowledge as human beings. Throughout my twenties, Cannabis protected me from suicide from my raging alcoholism. Because I adored weed so much at first, it tempered my alcoholism so that I did not outright kill myself. Had I not been obsessed with weed, I would most likely be dead by now via alcoholic cirrhosis.

Drugs have outlived their purpose in my life. I had become greedy and stopped practicing temperance and moderation after the first two years. I made taking drugs a lifestyle, becoming a drug addict by choice. I lost the ability to moderate after the first two years, and I now know it that I will never return to it. I also wish I had not smoked pot or experimented with any drugs until I was twenty-five years old. That is the official age the brain stops the cycle of neurological development and ceases growing. Drugs consumed me by the age of 23. They held me back from my full potential in life for eight long years. Still, drugs consistently gave me enough euphoria to trick me into seeing benefits that had long since dissipated through my frightful and excessive chemical self-indulgence. Now through total abstinence, I apply the lessons I learned from marijuana and other mind-altering substances regarding self-control, creativity, and empathy. I refuse to entertain a return to using, as I recall the dark ending to my drinking. I keep memories of my end-stage using from 2018 to 2020 firmly planted in my mind.

As Sebastian Horsley put it best (Horsley, 1), the irony of the drug lifestyle and experience begins as a genuine longing for mystical experiences, consciousness expansion, fun, sociability, and exploration. But the person in the early stages of drinking and using observes that without self-control over the amount and frequency of drugs or alcohol consumed, responsibility, and adherence to prioritizing their goals over their behaviors, the drug-taking experience **ONLY** ends sordidly alone and broken inside. Addicts always prioritize behaviors over their goal, which increases both depression and the underlying excuses to continue using long after the magic is gone, and denial is all that remains. Coldly, staring miserably at a wall in a comfortably euphoric, empty, and lonely prison that no one should ever have to experience (Horsley, 1). But I did experience this world at the end of my using career. There are no words in any language to describe the experience of addiction when the addict's tolerance gets high enough other than a living hell! Compared to the living heaven you initially experience with a low tolerance. Then, using and drinking or any addictive behavior is all about staving off boredom, shivering sickness, tolerance, and withdrawal. The fun evaporates, and you cannot even recognize yourself in the mirror because you are not yourself at all. Caught in the vicious cycle of substance abuse, a demonic imposter hell-bent on self-destruction and deception takes over; living from hit to hit and living for nothing and no-one else.

It is not drugging in and of itself that is the worst sin of all. We have sick pedophiles covered up by trusted religious institutions, mass genocides, school shootings, and power-hungry liars gaining totalitarian control over nations to top this. However, becoming addicted to drugs (or any unhealthy behavior) and letting psychoactive chemicals determine your identity and your happiness; this is where the convincing sin lies! Throughout human history (Hari, 2016) recreational drug use was responsible for many artistic and scientific achievements by those self-disciplined enough to possess self-control. Without self-control, drugs can so quickly become a life destroyer, showing you a nasty side of human nature, that none should ever have to experience. Because of the seemingly extreme pleasure of psychoactive chemicals when you start with a low tolerance, only the strongest of the strong avoid passing over that invisible line which separates the recreational user from the out-of-control alcoholic or drug addict. I would not wish my last three years of poly-drug addiction on a person who might attempt to murder my family in front of me! It was that sordid and ugly!

When I smoked Cannabis, I remember that music sounded utterly ethereal, an entirely mind-blowing experience that flowed from the walls, the sky, the streets, from within my soul. For the first time in 21 years, I was finally happy and comfortable in my own skin! It was artificial comfort that took years to let go. Through sobriety, I have finally found genuine comfort inside of myself. Earlier, I would have taken any dangerous method of feeling comfortable because of the psychological and spiritual war that raged within me. As a teenager, sobriety was not pleasant at all for me. I was constantly at odds with myself, and the world. I felt like the world was evil and corrupt and I became a drug addict to stay in touch with beauty instead of letting the repulsiveness of the world corrupt my spirit. Ironically, at the end when I nearly submitted to permanent, final slavery, the drug experience taught me demoralization and the dampening of my spiritual energy. I broke my shackles in 2020 and God willing will never return! But at 21, doing drugs for the first time, the world at last made sense to me, and I did not give a fuck about any future consequences back then. No one would have changed my mind when I was 21, as I was hell-bent on self-medicating and escaping by **ANY** means necessary. During that period, I believed that drugs gave me an escape and release better than anything else. I thought that **NOTHING** could compare! It seemed to me that drugs were my solution to life from the age of 20 to 29, **NOT** my problem!

From my point of view, it was a preposterous notion that drugs could become a problem for me! I could finally talk to girls without fear or impunity or care about rejection; food tasted like a living orgasm. Psychedelic visions surrounded me, and everything looked bright, profound, new, and untouched. Even the most mundane and stupid activities were suddenly fun and exciting for hours on end! It seemed like sacred medicine to soothe my brain and revitalize the senses into a 4K existence! Whereas before, my life was only shades of gloomy gray, now the colors had returned full bore! I believed I had found the elixir of life, drugs at 21 were my great panacea to all human ills, the penultimate solution to all my problems!

CHAPTER 5

HIGHWAY SOUL TRAIN-ROBBERY

I HAD THE PERFECT OPPORTUNITY TO TEST DRIVE MY NEWFOUND solution to life once I briefly joined a fraternity in college. I was driving back from one of my off-campus classes towards my university, shakily sober with a quarter ounce of weed in my trunk. My smudged sunglasses blocked none of the sun's harsh rays, as these beams illuminated the sidewalks packed with methamphetamine peddlers. Second-hand tires stacked mile high, and piles of litter polluted every block. I was caught in miles of traffic in my 2012 tricked-out Honda Accord. I was blasting "Origin of Symmetry" at full volume to get some gas after routinely driving 80 miles back and forth to visit my family. I was lost in the melodic majesty of Muse's magnum opus "Origin of Symmetry" grooving to the "Micro Cuts" track.

The Ecstasy ravers, fraternity drinkers, alcoholics, coked-out sorority girls, hippies, weed heads, beatniks, tweakers, addicts, and college town citizens alike realized that the authorities in the region were utterly incompetent and reviled in their pathological uselessness. This passivity created a comfortable illusion of normality that enabled the community to promote a lifestyle of self-destructive excess. The message to these college kids was abundantly clear. Laws were off the table! Take a drink until the drink takes you to your grave or inside somebody's pants. Take any drug within a five-inch radius and chase them down like assorted candy. Party your vital organs into a state of trashed, wasted and defeated submission while having regular, no condom sex with anything containing a pulse. The fraternity and sorority motto were always: *If you were not getting high, drunk, loaded, or laid, you were not worth anything worthwhile.*

Later the same day, I experienced a crisp fall evening on campus. I had just finished a regular workout at the gym, which included sessions on the ab roller, jump rope, and ultimate Frisbee. I am a self-professed obsessive-compulsive maniac in general. I bench-pressed and crunched my way into a shiny, glistening twelve pack, but could not slip into a mental jean jacket that presented any self-confidence or a remote sense of self-assurance despite being one of the students with the highest grades on campus. A few days prior, a blind student's advice was, "fake it till you make it," as he guzzled whiskey shots for breakfast. I sat on a bench smack dab in the middle of the quad, hating myself and the neighboring people. I had recently lost my virginity but felt an utterly nonexistent increase in my self-confidence or game with women. My confidence had sunk like the Titanic, and I was open to hanging out with lower companions who I could reliably share, commiserate, and revel in my misery with.

Contrary to my profoundly misguided beliefs, having sex did not solve any of my problems. All the bodily health in the world could not hide nor juxtapose the toxic, self-flagellating thoughts flowing through my fractured mind. My existential pain was second only to my confusion and abject horror at the surrounding individuals' mentality. Shallow pursuits were the authority and ruler over college school spirits. Wasted rush couples walked arm in arm, covered in puke stains and sold alongside fraternity shirts during rush season. They were all either, drinking or recovering from the previous night's drunkenness, stains of beer and leftover pepperoni pizza on their shirts from a fresh post-coital breakfast. They were drunkenly hurling vomit into nearby trash cans as they spoke about the fine art of butt-sex using exotic vegetables and produce; the conversation passing through sets of apathetic eardrums who knew this was par for the course. If a week passed at my university without someone puking on the quad, taking off someone's pants, or overdosing, the community knew the sky would rain money. A circumstance none of these students would achieve, let alone me during this time. Another student, thick shaggy blond curly hair with headphones the size of King Kong's fists, his sapphire blue eyes constantly glazed over, whizzed by on his skateboard. He rode with speed past me as I threw myself into a sober pity party. Little did I know he was looking for crack cocaine.

The only thought racing about in my fractured mind was that I was far too sober for a Friday night, and it was time to fix this issue with the utmost haste. I returned to the dormitory after chugging several swigs from a hidden bottle of rum I had stashed in the trunk of my car. The residence overflowed with crooked, meat-headed jocks, and I profoundly hated them all. They drank beer like mountain spring water routinely, and if sober, they would load up on so many energy drinks, they would start fights with anyone if they sniffed at them wrong. If you had a bicycle, it did not matter how expensive your lock was or how many hours you spent affixing a secure lock to your set of wheels. That ride was getting stolen at the first opportunity to be pawned for beer and narcotics. The jock fraternities, who hit on every woman within a two-inch radius, preferred to address any man who did not hit on every girl he saw with the sentimental label, "pussy-whipped bitch." They drank alcohol by the caseload and would overflow every bathroom in the dormitory with empty cans of blatant alcoholism. Every stall was drenched in gargantuan layers of urine, landing artfully everywhere but the toilet seat. The sinks were practically invisible beneath used condoms and dirty pubic hairs. Some would even add the alcoholic content from their vomit into their red plastic cups of beer if they could not afford more alcohol or abused cocaine and Adderall to "keep the colors at full mast." College partygoers aptly labeled these rituals "suicide contests."

I was an honor student with grades in the top 1% of the university who found solace in the library studying English and Psychology for hours, and averse to sniffing any hint of sports outside of baseball or ultimate Frisbee marathons. I drank as much or more than any of the fraternities did. A blonde hair, blue eyed guy once challenged me to a drinking contest. Here was a colossal mistake. I drank him under the table, then accordingly drank myself under the table and broke his furniture as a gesture of defiant contempt. My standard alcoholic intake at twenty-one comprised countless red solo cups of beer, chugging fifths of vodka, and spiced rum by the 100-proof bottle every weekend, not to mention more than double the average intake of the disgraceful caffeine and alcohol combination. This consumption had become nightly practice by the time I was 22, a ritual that reduced my social skills to the aptitude of a lobotomized chimpanzee. My philosophy in this environment near the constant proximity of drugs was the product of a one-track mentality consumed in pain and self-doubt. "The quicker and more incapacitating the substance, all the better." My weekdays were primarily comprised of making A's and B's in every class while violently shaking like a hungover leaf blower with a busted motor. I cured my debilitating shakes and sweating through self-flagellating nightly blackout drinking only two years into my drinking career, with social drinking a distant memory. I would begin drinking heavier and heavier for years until I put down the bottle for good and my drug habits tapered off, having learned through bitter experiences that I am one of those people who cannot moderate my consumption. I nearly died countless times before I learned my lesson about abusing narcotics.

CHAPTER 6

MASTER THESIS IN MARIJUANA & MAYHEM

IT WAS THE NIGHT OF THE ANNUAL CEREMONY, A PARTY HELD BY THE honor majors on campus once each year. The highlight, a drugged-out festival of the season, and all the students knew it. This group of remarkable students, all 4.0 honor roll students who designed custom majors using the universities' pre-existing curriculum. Nearly every student had made the honor roll, and they all had a master's degree summa cum laude in partying and drug experimentation. I immediately gravitated towards this crowd because of their intelligence and work ethic, as most were opposed to the fraternities' hard-drinking antics. I had just discovered the wonders of Cannabis, albeit from the same crowd. The counterculture was in full bloom on the campus. Long hallways covered in spray-painted graffiti featured posters of naked women which adorned the tie-dye textural patterns on the walls. Bob Marley emblems on every floor, with every dorm room engulfed in the distinctive aroma of weed smoke. The cops never stopped for long the overflowing tidal waves of drugs flowing through the college desert strip. If the cops ever arrested a drug dealer, no one was even remotely fazed, as a new drug dealer with better dope would replace them in milliseconds. A narcotics trader had set up shop for the evening. He dealt with LSD, Adderall, cocaine, heroin, and pounds of marijuana straight from the dormitories. His customers ranged from those who majored in environmental studies, prodigious potheads; honor roll students shooting up blow cut with drain cleaner, to super senior burnouts who ate blotter acid for supper at all hours of the night.

This narcotics trader differed from other drug hustling types in his attuned fashion sense. He wore a fleece-lined jean jacket, complete with zippered pockets to keep his weed stash secure. Not that he would need to hide it. I stumbled into the lobby, already staggering, and drunk as a skunk. I had finished my leftover bottle of spiced rum and pilfered five bottles of beer from a passed-out sorority girl. The girl had wealthy parents, so there was always beer in her fridge. She loved nothing more than wearing skin-tight clothing while hooking up with several frat boys to display confidence in her image, drinking herself into a coma every night until she would hook up using the same tired lie, "I'm on birth control!" She would sleep with any man who had a bar tab or a fake I. D and had developed a notorious reputation around the sorority circuit in my college as "the Quickie Queen." Despite her promiscuities, this woman was far from unintelligent. She was the annual chairperson of her sorority. She had donated hundreds of dollars to charitable causes, combining a bachelor's in environmental science, with a minor in Environmental Policy Management. Her dream was to become a solar cell technician. Her philanthropic vision became progressively harder to maintain as her drinking and using steadily spiraled out of control. Not that she was anywhere near my league, swimming Olympian laps in the highball glass or sampling assorted narcotics. I entered the dorm, Primus blasting on a surround sound stereo. Several students were celebrating top marks on their midterms by sparking up ganja blunts in the hallways. I was right at home.

I lurched into the dealers' room, already so loaded that I was having trouble standing up or forming coherent sentences. The gang was all present as I polished off two of my five hijacked beer bottles and struggled not to fall through an open window onto the sidewalk. The dealer was busy smoking a joint next to another student, a music major who combined his love of music with anthropology. His goal was to create music mixing heightened social awareness with binaural beats to induce trance-like states of consciousness in his audiences. He remained stoned off his gourd and in a business model of partying until you overdose. Eyes bloodshot red, he had the innate ability to laugh at a marathon of YouTube cat memes as if they were the secret of eternal youth. Standing next to him were two drunken sorority girls dancing from an old BOSE speaker to Katy Perry, lip-syncing the vocals to "Roar" as the dealer rolled up a carton of fresh marijuana joints. One of these girls was nearly seven feet tall, with a sandy blonde hairstyle and emerald-green bloodshot eyes. She wore a bra strap so poorly constructed that she had to keep retying the sash as it fell off her continuously. If she had been dancing topless, not one student would bat an eye.

Some students would even masturbate in the hallways while drunk on tequila, as a fraternity hazing ritual. The fraternities at this college had no problem overcharging students ten to twenty dollars apiece to get into their exclusive parties. They did this in order to have the money they needed to have bodyguards who steered other students away from the best women, bottles of smuggled liquor, and drugs, keeping these for themselves. Not that this stopped anyone from getting loaded or laid! I was a saber-tooth tiger of drunken stoned madness; no restrictions could remotely hold me. I somehow never felt I gained a tolerance for the stuff because the first drink or drug did me in every time. My burgeoning PTSD magnified with every glass or hit I took, but the numbed disinhibition and euphoria I received from alcohol and drugs made it increasingly easy to rationalize my self-destructive excesses.

The other girl was at the beginning of a drunken buzz. She was short and portly, but attractive, nonetheless. She had long flowing purple eyelashes, dimples the size of craters, an ample waist, hundreds of ripped holes in her jeans, thick curves, penetrating brown eyes, and a golden smile. Next to a wooden table covered with ashes, roaches, and cigarette butts were several shot glasses of vodka, an entire bottle of gin, and three large plastic zip-lock bags filled with top-shelf weed. The short girl was enjoying herself as she belted out, "I GOT THE EYE OF THE TIGER!!! DANCING THROUGH THE FIRE!!! YOU'RE GONNA HEAR ME ROAR!!!" Not that I cared to be subtle towards females while staggeringly drunk, high, and unable to take my eyes off the mountain of weed on the table. I focused my eyes with a look of sarcastic contempt to hide my insecurities. "Katy Perry is a dry, shallow, pre-packaged, pop-star clone. Listening to her manufactured, processed cheese, you might as well replace your headphones with elephant shit because it will sound less disgusting." The sorority girls did not appreciate my shamefaced candor, grabbing their whiskey shots off the table to drink their pain of poor musical taste away. Each lady took a swig of liquor. Dimple Queen could hold her liquor well, taking two shots back-to-back with little noticeable effect. The tall woman stood up unsteadily as she took one more shot, then began convulsing. Being hammered at this moment, I could guess that I would need new pants at some time during the evening's debauchery. The tall girl swayed back and forth with the look of a deer caught in the headlights. "Huh guys, I don't think this one went down so well." She swayed, looking like she was about to face plant. We all braced for impact. I was too drunk to brace for anything. Within seconds, she had puked all over my jeans, a cocktail of whiskey, beer, and leftover quesadillas; she passed out on the floor in a display of grace and poise.

The drug dealer ignored the drunken girls because he knew what I wanted just from the look in my eyes. I struggled not to vomit myself from the puke covering my pants. He knew I needed to smoke high-grade marijuana to counteract the tsunami of destructive blackout drunkenness I had created and to counter my inevitable propensity when drunk, to break any object within two feet of me. "Are you looking for an ounce of OG Kush, my man?" My mouth watered harder than a starving man dying of thirst, and I bought a fat sack with no regrets. I looked around the room in wonder, a giant poster of Bob Marley flapping heroically beneath an industrial dormitory fan, but my attention quickly shifted to the massive glass bong staring directly at me. The dealer, always the observant party leader, called out to me, "So freshman, you ever take a fat bong rip?" Already hammered and so wasted, my eyes were darting back and forth with the elegance of smashed F1 formula racers. I was unable to walk two feet in any direction without property damage; therefore I was more than open to new experiences. So, the dealer took out a thick nug of weed, using a serrated blade to slice off a nice chunk of the bud. Unfolding a small pouch containing hashish, he loaded up the chalice of the glass bong with flakes of bubble hash atop the weed, creating a massive grass tortilla. He then flaunted his master's knowledge of effective pot smoking. "This is Afghan hash I got from my dawg in Ontario! The hash that clocks in at 60% THC! I guarantee one hit will shoot your brain out of a cannon into a higher plane of spiritual existence!"

I needed no further encouragement and wrapped my lips around the chalice. "Now remember homie, hold in that medicine for as long as possible. Do not be a bitch and choke! Whatever you do, don't swallow the bong water; it doesn't wash down well with cheap beer." I was too drunk to laugh at the irony of this statement as I threw caution to cyclonic winds and inhaled a massive toke of marijuana and Afghan hash. The smoke swirled about in my lungs, sinking down my throat in a dessert of bong water milkshake. I held in the smoke for as long as possible but noticed my breath visibly straining. "Dude, what the fuck?! Spit out the bong water, you nut job!!!" the dealer screamed, concerned that he would have to clean up a stadium-sized pool of bong water residue, mixed delicately with Captain Morgan's spiced vomit icing. I was a proud nonconformist, so I swallowed all the bong water, and ten seconds of constant weed smoke erupted from my lungs, exhaling a Snoop Dogg genie cloud of Kush!

The smoke was thick, and the aroma was overpowering, pot haze intermingling across every surface of the walls. Marijuana smoke was floating into the fabric of every Bob Marley flag in all the rooms off the dorm hall. I both cherish and loathe this memory because I romanticized this moment many years into my addiction. I saw this as the way I wanted to live, as did everyone around me in the atmosphere of hedonistic escapism. I have only recently realized the emptiness and despondency I felt in those hallways.

I coughed hard for ten seconds, yet I felt great! For the next three minutes, I became convinced that I had inhaled enough smoke to give the entire dorm a contact high. There was so much weed smoke in the room now. The passed-out sorority girl awoke from her drunken coma and was coughing more violently than I was, given that I was the one who swallowed a liter of bong water. Suddenly, the drunken sorority girls looked significantly more attractive as I melted into a nearby couch. Everything felt fantastic as I announced with baked glee. "I'm higher than a kite orbiting the rings of Saturn!" The other students were not paying attention to my stoned candor because of more significant concerns. "Fuck, when's the debauchery going to begin? I need to crawl my way into horny females with hairy jungles down south. This condom smeared in a bathtub of Astro glide will not wear itself." "Patience young Padawan." the drug dealer reassured the stoned entourage, "the night is young, and if you have the connections, you will get lots of fresh pussy." A well-known bunch of frat boys came driving by our tripping, drunk, and smoked-out dorm. They were well known around the fraternity circuit as sex fiends and perpetual players. Their twisted philosophy towards all relationships was a consistent ritual of convincing girls to drink copious amounts of Jack

Daniels shots back-to-back until the girl was willing to take her clothes off followed by a pump and dump. Several other students were riding shotgun right alongside him in his Mustang GT. A drunken entourage squished between leather seats caked in whiskey. All were approaching the comatose drunk stage. The leader, a ginger-haired broad-shouldered gentleman, always the straight man, blurted out, "Hey, you ever ride broke-back on an 800-pound mountain gorilla's pussy?" I replied somewhat hesitantly. "Not yet. It's on my to-do list." He was not one to give up on me, especially while shamefaced out of his mind and surrounded by lushes. "Come to Vegas with us and you'll get ridden by the horniest gorilla pussy in town!" He chugged his beer down to the bottom of the pint glass without spilling a drop of poison and drove off, swerving across several lanes.

I became extremely uncomfortable at the statement I had made a few seconds earlier. Feeling paranoid and very stoned, I took this opportunity to apologize to the drunk girls as I poured myself three more shots of vodka and downed them in a flash. I explained to them I was bitter because I was burned out from a combination of studying like a maniac and subconsciously nursing a multitude of growing addictions. Not to mention, I was flirting with death under the influence of five beers, a ton of pot smoke, three shots of vodka, and half a fifth of Captain Morgan. Dimple Queen smiled at me and my red bloodshot eyes as we danced to "Jammin'" blasting out of the BOSE setup. Music had never sounded so amazing to me, as the weed and alcohol combination magnified the intensity of every note. By the time Bob Marley's "African Herbsman" was playing, the room felt like it was visibly glowing with the communal spirit of Rastafarianism. I felt like I was in Jamaica and never wanted to leave. No one batted an eye at this orgy of intoxication, as everyone on the second floor had followed our lead and were blazing perpetual joints and fully loaded blunts cut with cocaine. As several students engaged in a game of beer pong in the next hallway and the honor students were pre-gaming next to them (pre-gaming refers to consuming enough alcohol and drugs to get a buzz on without getting intoxicated enough to want to sober up), I was about to take a "Blow" inspired unforgettable ride through the bottom of hell.

One of the dorm leaders excelled. He was a music major who maintained a 4.0 GPA in in all his classes, even receiving a scholarship from a state university to further his studies in music theory and composition. He did not need a job, however, because he had found his full-time career as the next John Lennon during his Yoko Ono period. He was eating LSD by the sheet, smoking pounds of weed, flipping out on psilocybin mushrooms, and snorting cocaine cut with ether while performing for crowds in the nude. His parents had paid for his college tuition over the eight years; he could invent any excuse to remain, semester after semester. He lied to his parents about failing grades to keep the party going for the rest of his life. He remained ambivalent about his college major while smoking weed like cigarettes, snorting cocaine as a substitute for oxygen, and eating strips of windowpane acid by the sheet for eight years. He played in a local jam band known as "The Butthole Strippers." All five members were potheads, coke whores, junkies, and seasoned acid freaks. "The Butthole Strippers" spliced mashups of psychedelic rock, grunge, and reggae tunes dipped into an overflowing vat of psycho juice. Regardless of the drugs, his band always turned up tremendous crowds at every party where they jammed, given this dorm leader's propensity to appear on stage drugged out and naked.

I noticed a common theme in this college community. All the students who grappled the most with substance abuse were near the top of the class. The ones who earned the highest grades also struggled the hardest in developing a stable, self-actualized identity for themselves, making them far more predisposed to self-abusive excesses. I subscribe to the belief that intelligent people have a greater susceptibility to addiction than stupid individuals because genetics often curse geniuses, and intellects suffer from constant overthinking spells that make self-destructive habitual numbness increasingly attractive, despite the inevitable consequences. Some students avoided drugs, wearing DARE t-shirts, and labeling everyone who partied as a loser. However, approximately half of them could not maintain an average grade of a C or above. One student custom majored in biology and Astrophysics. He would keep his academic record high by recklessly mainlining speed-ball cocktails of amphetamines and hydromorphone for days on end. The walls in his dorm were covered in a conglomerate of post-it notes featuring humorous anecdotes. "You will have plenty of time to retire when you're dead and buried." and "A broken clock has the wisdom of the elders, for it needs no time to achieve; time is an illusion." Another student had maintained A's and B's, hoping to become a major in communications. This goal became derailed after he was introduced to opiates, namely smoking heroin. He switched to majoring in chemistry, which supported his ever-growing habit and gave him newfound abilities to synthesize his own bags of drugs. Several girls were dating him, mainly to get access to his China White heroin supply, unadulterated purity, and potency twice that of Black Tar heroin.

I had just moved into the chemistry major's dorm hall where he lived, as another joint was getting passed around, filled with Sour Diesel mixed in with White Widow. After several hits of the Cannabis joint, my brain seemed like it was plastered on the peripheral walls of the galaxy. Bob Marley smiled and waved at me as "Buffalo Soldier" played triumphantly in the background. It was as if all the world's problems did not remotely matter at all when we were drinking and using. I was surrounded by constant partying, rivers of drugs, and relatively useless authority figures, all shrouded in a valley of total madness.

I admired this chemistry major's ambition given the field of study he pursued, though I was unaware that his habit was the underlying motivation for his change of major. Yet I was already in the process of slowly changing my goals to match my drug intake, as I already was a habitual weekend warrior, smoking weed and getting drunk every weekend without hesitancy. He did not care, already slurring his speech in between nodding out. "Yo sophomore, I packed an extra bowl just for you. Take a fat toke." I looked down at his desk and noticed several packets of tinfoil and piles of aluminum with burn stains all over, an unsettling chill snaking down my spine. Just then, the stoner entourage walked by his dorm in a cloud of weed smoke. They were quick to point out disparagingly that his bowl was laced. "Don't smoke those bowls, not even a single hit. He always spikes his marijuana with heroin and cocaine speedballs now." Our chemistry major's retort? "Except that speed balling is what all the cool kids are doing. Don't you want to become cool?" I gave him the benefit of the doubt and passed the bowl he packed back to him, running away like hell into the middle of the hallway, where I found an unguarded pot brownie. After drinking a gallon of fountain water, I lapped up the brownie like a starving wolverine, only for one student to notice the brownie was consumed. "Oh, wow... dude, you just ate an edible with 80% pure THC; you will get completely faded tonight!" Stoned off my gourd and approaching sorority formal drunk before I ate said brownie, I knew I would have an outstanding experience or go off the rails. It is always a roll of the dice concerning drug misuse, and the results are seldom favorable. The ironic cosmic trick of drug addiction is that drugs are a ton of fun at the start, but by the time consequences become part of the druggy lifestyle, you have created a pattern of conditioning and reinforcement that many never break out of!

All I could think about was how I could get hard narcotics with the ease of ordering a slice of pizza. Supporting research from the Carnegie Endowment for International Peace and syndicated columnist Moisés Naím confirms illegal drugs are easier to get than legal drugs (Naím, 168). Seventy-one percent of Americans believe that *The War on Drugs* has failed, yet only 19% of people think global drug policy should shift from detainment and incarceration to medication and rehabilitation (Naím, 168). This split in public opinion has led to an argument no one in public policy wants to look at. Naím's research contended that America's inability to think logically about drug policy has inadvertently allowed the nation to become the world's largest importer of illegal narcotics and the number one exporter of punitive drug policies (Naím, 169).

I enjoyed Cannabis tremendously but had no desire to do heroin and never tried smack (not that this stopped me from getting addicted to opiates later, as I already depended on painkillers and benzodiazepines for sleep). My decision was sufficiently reinforced by staring at the chemistry major's pale skin, with his pinpoint eyes seemingly bulging out of their sockets. Every other day his entourage offered me smack or cocaine. They lived the lifestyle of part-time college students and full-time cocaine addicts, smack heads and hustlers.

This student whose studies focused on narcotics was correct in his assertion that a pot brownie's effects added to an aperitif of drunkenness would have added to the buzz exponentially. I was now so high that the effects were impossible to ignore. All the cartoon murals on the walls appeared to be swaying, mingling, and dancing independently. To my field of vision, a Velvet Underground poster merged with another poster of Jerry Garcia. They created a hybrid, with Garcia's beard caught in between the Velvet Underground banana logo. The banana repeatedly began peeling itself. It was breathtaking, significantly, because the murals were reshaping themselves in perfect synchronization with the music. I took this as a sign that I needed to come down a little before the party started, and I went outside to the quad for some fresh air.

The night was still as ice, and I walked in silence amidst tall groves of palm trees and manicured lawns smothered in radioactive fertilizer. My eyes became red as a tomato as I investigated the night sky, glowing brightly with ethereal stars. I wondered in my mind if anyone felt as lonely as I did that night, struggling to keep my mind from falling apart, yet feeling happy and centered in a fucked-up way. In this world of insanity, I felt at home because I found people who had something to escape from, like myself. I could not stop drinking, fraternity party or not, rationalizing because my thought process was that "drinking will help me talk to people more." Conversations at parties for an active alcoholic mostly involved swaggering up trashed, anti-authoritarian and belligerent. If someone had a drink lying around, I would help myself to any leftover glasses whether they were in someone's hands or not. I needed that drink and liquid courage far more than I needed others approval. If I approached women, my game would compromise of farting, sweating like a thousand camels roasting to death in the Sahara Desert, and vomiting where I pleased because I was too drunk to form coherent sentences. I would usually introduce myself through the universal language of slurred speech, puke, and blackouts after hugging the toilet for seven hours on an average night. Drugs became more and more attractive to me over alcohol, because at first, I could socialize without the negative psychical effects or apparent impairments to my cognitive process.

Meanwhile, in my new marijuana mental meadow, the sky was covered in rotating hexagons, which changed colors every few seconds, revealing the full color spectrum. My color theory teacher would be so proud. I knew this batch of marijuana was just the right amount of potent. I wondered if I would ever come down but received my answer all too soon that the utter madness was only just beginning. In the middle of the quad, I saw six college students passing around an oddly shaped pipe and a stem. At first, I thought they were smoking weed, but this illusion was destroyed quickly. They were all smoking crack cocaine openly in the middle of the quad. I looked in absolute shock and horror at the man who passed on his hit of crack as he foamed violently at the mouth. His eyes were vacant and empty of all soul or expression, glazed pools of silver blackness with nearly nonexistent pupils. The kid could not have been a day over 25, yet he looked more wrinkled, torn up, and scarred than a 90-year-old cruising down dementia lane. His skin was as pale white as a ghost, covered in scabs, and his nose was glazed over with white cocaine powder. A young mind lost in the insatiable hunger for white specks. Face to face with mortality, this student was unphased by his haggard appearance as he took a massive blast of crack. Holding in his hit of rock for a full twenty seconds, he exhaled an enormous cloud of white billowing smoke that blanketed the entire sky as he walked over to me, coked out of his mind. I attempted to absorb the insanity in front of me while still stoned off my gourd from a huge bong rip, drunk as hell, and tripping my face off from a laced brownie.

He was upfront with me now, high as a kite. "Hey man, you want to smoke some crack?!" I immediately said, "NO!" "Your loss, man," he replied, as he flashed a psychotic grin. Half of his teeth were missing. The kid then took another massive rip of crack, and then he decided there would be no more sharing his rock cocaine for the night. He hopped on his K15 skateboard as the other five crack smokers stood in dead silence, staring at nothing but the stem in his hand. I believed one false move from this student while cracked out, and the other base heads would tackle him and grab the stash. Crackheads are not like potheads. They will not allow you to savor the effects before they demand their next hit. Not that this occurred, as the kid hopped on his skateboard and launched himself straight into an oak tree. His skull was fractured and gushed over with blood dripping down his neck as the poor wretch sprawled out on the grass unconscious. Not once did his crack pipe or the rock cocaine ever release from his grip; even after his shirt was ripped open by an adjacent branch as he went unconscious, the crack was firmly grasped in his fist. The other students rushed to assist their fallen comrade by prying his hands open and grabbing his stem filled with a rock. Before I could even blink, all five of the remaining base heads had scattered in all directions like they had red fire ants shoved up their pants, leaving me staring at an unconscious crack connoisseur wondering if I would survive the night. I figured now was as good a time as ever to move towards the basement and blend in with the crowd, which would be easier than basic arithmetic. Given that everyone at this moment had no conception of what sobriety was integration would be a piece of cake. Reaching the dorm, I had not walked a few feet before two students intercepted me. "Dude, there's a killer jazz concert going on in the basement, and all the girls are ripe for sex," He announced this as casually as ordering a ham sandwich on rye bread with mayonnaise. We walked down a small set of stairs, filled with anti-establishment graffiti tags scrawled upon every cinder block, such as "Fuck the Police," "Question Authority," and "Smoke Weed Every Day."

Meanwhile, back in malevolent hangover inducing reality, the hard liquor and fistfuls of beer I had for dinner wanted to leave the lavish resort of my stomach lining. In response, I puked a lake of Jewish vomit all over a nearby torn-up couch. The chemistry major remained calm. "Don't worry about that couch. No one sits on it because several nomadic students who live off intravenous truckloads of meth and PCP had doggy-style sex on it, and cum stains have been in the cushions for nearly a year." My entire conception of reality at this moment was disfigured beyond repair. The level of drug use on campus seemed to exist as an out-of-control tsunami that only grew. I had come from a high school where teenagers were expelled for possession of even a single joint. Now I lived in a sea of alcoholic cops and wave upon wave of skinny honor students strung out on narcotic landfills. Not that I would let this notion impede me from making a complete ass of myself that night. There was a tray of cookies sitting on a table next to me and I had no clue if they were laced with THC or not. While fraternity boys and hippies alike were drunk as fuck, trying to get laid. I wolfed down the cookies like a jackal to stuff down the pain of my loneliness. Dozens of women were talking to random people, and all I could feel was strange. I did not have the same desire to drink my brains out when enough mind-altering substances were in me to counteract the effects of being drunk alone, probably because of the strength of the hash and the brownie. I would smile at all the women to project a confidence, which I did not have. I was a Ferrari with no license to drive at 21. Young, brilliant, but severely broken from abuse. Riddled with hallucinogenic PTSD from adolescent experiences and knee-deep in the bottle, I was already approaching the brink of suicidal tendencies; sleep without liquor or narcotics had already become near impossible.

A jazz ensemble had begun in the basement of the dorm, the walls decked out in beautiful leather and spruced up with Cannabis leaves. Just then, I saw one student naked on the scene, with his dick hanging out like an exclamation point. It was a massive penis, appearing in my current mindset to stretch the length of the room. His bush was untrimmed and remarkably dense reminding me of a Canadian pine forest in the summer season. I was both mortified that he was naked and impressed that he dared to perform while naked with no fear of the audience. Was he intoxicated or simply crazy? God save him if the man was sober in any way. He needed Thorazine, Lithium, and a strait jacket. Not that there was any desire for temperance or ANY self-control in the rock-star mind of this performer. His vocals combined raspy philosophies drenched in Syd Barrett's breakfast portion of LSD. Three new performers entered the stage, beginning a slow jazz waltz. All I remember is being too stoned and immediately going into freestyle dance in front of everyone. My mood seemed to lift correspondingly, floating on an expressway towards heaven with every song they played. So, I danced for about 5 hours that felt like 300 years. It was an incredible feeling. I had always been self-conscious about dancing. Stoned out of my mind, I felt free to improvise with half-baked moonwalking as I busted out a split with the poise of a drunken ballerina.

I left the room for a while to sit in the grass and reflect on my life. I was happy that I said no to crack and heroin. I was even more ecstatic that the weed high was still going strong. For the first time in my life, I looked at the sky and could see the constellations forming. The stars were twinkling in a burning, ethereal flame of passion and ecstasy in my bloodshot vision. Then, I realized I had a strong need to urinate, recognizing that there was no reason to pee on public property because I did not feel drunk. After handling my business (while smoking a bowl in the bathroom), I went on the prowl for other students who were around to join me in burning more marijuana. I approached a dorm room near the ladies' bathroom. A girl toppled out of the ladies' bathroom on top of me in the hallway. Her bare arms and legs were exposed, covered with obvious track marks and abscesses from head to toe. She was the eldest sister of one of the most popular and promiscuous students in the sorority. A brilliant student, she majored in zoology because she loved animals. She steadfastly believed animals were equal beings to humans. I am still waiting for a platypus to teach me how to pay my taxes yet hope springs eternal! She was one of the most active students in community service ventures, working at an animal rescue shelter nearly every day. She planned to write her graduating thesis on the rights of animals. However, she had been raped by one of the fraternity boys after he slipped her a cocktail laced with Rohypnol; a benzodiazepine with ten times the potency of Valium.

Correspondingly, she had turned to mainlining opiates to numb the pain. I was scared, never having encountered a strung-out student before. But I held no judgment of her junk habit. I lost the ability to do that without looking at how maddening my drinking already was. She also had a 4.0 GPA and was still maintaining her grades. Despite her excellent academic track record, I knew she was falling apart at the seams, and so was I, despite my unflagging denial. Deep abscesses were nestled inside her forearms, ornamented by a smattering of 28cc gauge needles in her skin she had not bothered to remove. Despite my drunkenness, I quickly grabbed each syringe in a state of panic and removed them from her pale skin. Then I performed CPR on her mouth. I somehow had revived her, without Naltrexone; an opioid antagonist used to counteract heroin overdoses. In fact, she did not shoot heroin, but OxyContin. She came from a wealthy family that could afford pharmaceutical heroin. Ironically, OxyCodone carries none of the stigma of heroin despite having the same chemical makeup. I was still aghast to see how a beautiful human being had become a scarred shell of herself, ripped into shreds and staring into the face of death. Little did I know that several years later, although I never used needles, I would fall in love with OxyContin and opiates. These were the same class of drugs that she had abused, and they provided the same oblivion—an obsession that nearly cost me my life.

I wondered what kind of work she could find, knowing full well the bad stigma intravenous drug use carried with it. According to BioMed Central's supporting research, stigma related to drug use is increases for female substance abusers. This stigma enhances gender and race-based stigmatization in both potential jobs and mental health care. The same rehabilitation clinics which demand increased healthcare for the mentally ill will deny or restrict access to people who suffer from substance abuse (Olphen et al.,2). Although the average time in jail for simple possession remains 45 days, even brief periods of incarceration have devastating effects on the lives of addicts. Saddled with a criminal record and the termination of medical benefits, including Medicaid, users suffer from reduced access to mental health treatment and increased recidivism rates in most patients, treated or untreated (Olphen et al.,3). According to further supporting research by Johann Hari, most users are forced into poverty through social and financial marginalization, surrounded by diseases that perpetuate their condition instead of treating it (Hari, 166). Addiction viewed through this perspective is an adaptation to one's environment. When the environment produces a feeling of powerlessness and isolation for an individual, addictive tendencies always increase. If the domain is loving and supportive, addictive vulnerabilities decrease (Hari, 293). The drug warriors aiming to punish addicts under the misguided belief this will eliminate addiction have designed a system with conditions that deepen addictive tendencies through the strict love approach (Hari, 174). The environment surrounding me in college was one of perpetually feeling isolated and alone. Therefore, the abuse of narcotics became as natural to me as breathing. Addicts are already well versed in self-loathing and self-flagellation to an unbearable extreme. The system does not need to stigmatize addicts or the mentally ill any more than such people already willingly engage in. Yet, the system does so anyway because profit is the primary motivator over health. Their goal is to convince the mentally ill and addicts that they cannot escape the revolving door of rehabilitation or institutions; they are powerless to change themselves or their lifestyles. Then those in power, who see addicts and alcoholics as walking cash dispensaries, reap all the benefits as the majority of users adopt an attitude of learned helplessness to please their superiors, and slip through the cracks.

CHAPTER 7

A MOMENT OF
FLEETING CLARITY

SEEING THIS POOR WOMAN'S SUFFERING MAY HAVE BEEN THE FIRST
moment of clarity I had regarding my choices. It did not last long because I was coming down,
and all I wanted in the world was to get a lot higher. I carried the now unconscious woman to
bed, then went back to the basement to get drunker and smoke more weed. Several juniors and
seniors offered to smoke me out for sharing an ounce of dank with them a few weeks prior.
I had *borrowed* the ounce of pot from my meth dealer roommate. Months ago, my roommate
kicked me out with his stash after dosing me with crystal meth in a neighboring college town.
This was his attempt to sober me up from my maintenance routine of beer and vodka. I did
not come down for three gloomy days of agony. I spent ten hours aimlessly wandering around
at a drunken party for what seemed like thirteen hours, only then remembering where I
had parked my car. Even then, I was still so out of it that while I was at the wheel, I allowed
hooligans to rob me of all that was in my trunk. Picking holes into my skin, hallucinating
bugs the size of volcanoes, three days of no sleep, and unable to get drunk on about forty beers
I 'd chugged, this was my first rock bottom. I did not sleep for three solid days and walked
around the party rooms, literally a tweaker zombie. The next day, I awoke feeling dead to
the universe, coming down from the meth, lifeless and pale, sitting in the backseat of my
car. I looked like death walking the Grim Reaper himself. I thank God every day that my
mother did not see me in that wretched state. She would have jumped off a bridge because I
did not look like her son, but a possessed demon from the bottom of hell. All my dopamine

was gone, my serotonin receptors pruned out of existence, and I wondered if I would ever trust anyone or anything again, especially myself. The meth set off an ugly, relentless, 5-year social paranoia that exacerbated all my borderline personality disorder symptoms for five long years after my college nightmare. I became afraid of interacting with people, increasingly paranoid, and soon preferred only to be social when I became super loaded.

Back in the dorms and still exceedingly high on weed, I sat with many fraternity boys. One student majored in biology and neuroscience. He was also a massive weed head, able to roll up blunts with a whole eighth of weed inside. Sometimes, he would even roll quarter ounce blunts with extra-large swisher sweets. The weed was only magnifying in intensity as I sampled his hashish-laced blunts. I wondered if I was ever coming down as we sat outside the dorm on a torn couch. Puke stains were blatantly clear, along with traces of fresh semen in the fabric lining. The cold desert wind rattled like a rattlesnake across our stoned faces. Another frat boy had just rolled up a blunt, and I got my answer. As we passed the blunt around to the left, getting progressively more stoned, two students revealed to me more of their checkered past. One started getting into weed and alcohol during college when his parents divorced. His alcoholic mother left his father and the remaining family destitute to hook up with a real estate agent. Another 4.0 student, excelling in mathematics, trigonometry, and astronomy, was held back several years because of a bust for cocaine trafficking a few years back. He told me he had not used cocaine in two years with the help of a marijuana maintenance program. Looking into his bloodshot eyes, I had little reason to doubt his intentions, finding that the more pot I smoked, the less alcohol I consumed, or I avoided drinking altogether initially.

By the end of my using career, I found that any substituting of one drug for another to avoid using my drugs of choice was impossible, as I had to use all of them to get the high, I craved. I was craving drugs to prevent the cravings of other drugs and there is no existence worse on Earth, then being trapped in this cycle of rationalizing the use of one addiction to overcome the use of another addiction. Weed today would quickly lead me to using all my favorite mind-altering agents because I could not feel right on a single drug alone today. I quickly discovered that on liquor, writing was impossible. Because I started Cannabis at 21, not during my adolescence when it would have had more detrimental effects, its neuroprotective properties allowed me to experience less cognitive impairment to my higher functioning and enhanced my senses. For those two golden years, weed increased my sensitivity to everyone and everything around me instead of desensitizing me. Naturally, this made me want to become a stoner and to be known as a weed head to everyone. I saw nothing wrong with being high all the time back then, but saw being high as an enhancement to all the activities I cared about, which marijuana once was. By the end, weed numbed me and impaired my senses and judgement just as badly as alcohol ever did. Unlike alcohol, I fought to accept this to the bitter end until denial was impossible. My experience has shown that everyone's behaviors with alcohol, drugs, and compulsive actions remain unique. Some can moderate successfully, others cannot and become addicts; they cannot undo crossing that invisible line no matter how many lies they tell themselves about their habits. They often must learn that lesson the hard way before they clean themselves up or die in the process!

One grad student found he was unable to find steady work despite receiving his bachelor's in mathematics because of his previous felony convictions for possession of heroin and methamphetamines. He took up a drug-dealing venture full time to supplement his income because he had no other career prospects with that mark on his record for life. He did not need to travel far to find hungry customers, distributing bags of weed, opiates, and cocaine to string out college addicts, stoners, and full-time party guerrillas along the coast. This formula alone allowed him to pay several months rent and all his debts in a single swoop. He worked with several dealers in rotation, concealing the drugs in mysterious hiding places all over the dorms. Sometimes they would stash weed underneath the toilet, and whenever someone said, "I need to plant green logs," this was the cue for quarter grams and ounces to pop out of the cabinets like a Jack-in-the-box!

The cops had intimidated the grad student by threatening him with twelve years in prison for dealing several ounces of cocaine on his first bust. Even so, once he snitched on his previous wholesale heroin, meth and coke hustlers, the cops let him out on intensive probation as an informant, to which he responded by locating another wholesale drug dealer. This pusher had far better security precautions against a bust having begun evolving his distribution platform from local sales to the online Dark net. They began raking in seemingly endless marijuana, heroin, speed, and cocaine profits. Weed smoke became the very essence of the hallways, marijuana smoke floating through the ventilation shafts, intoxicating an endless supply of college greenhorns, who guzzled liquor shots for their substitute supply of oxygen. It was clear to all of us that *The War on Drugs* had failed. I honestly questioned the validity of *The War on Drugs* and its effects on access to narcotics. Prohibition, everyone could see, was an abysmal failure. Every few seconds, I would stumble across burnt spoons left out in the open within adjacent hallways. Burnt spoons filled with the pungent smell of raw vinegar—the acrid smell of cooking heroin on the stove. Syringes left exposed in opened drawers next to the pot dealers' dorms, scattered like silverware down poetic puke-filled hallways, dripping with madness and the chaotic trials of youth.

At this very moment, I was high and drunk, with easy access to every class of narcotics under the sun. For all this grad student's academic abilities, his felony record would likely mean he could never work a regular job again. His previous convictions eliminated his options to earn or live any semblance of an ordinary life without dealing drugs. If he was busted for mainlining hydromorphone, he knew his parents would cut him off, even without knowing that he sold narcotics in order to take more narcotics for free. Despite his excellent grades, his parents hypocritically insisted on a zero-tolerance policy towards drug use. However, both his parents were active alcoholics themselves, downing bottles of whiskey and gin every night like they were Coors Light. The grad student heavily increased his hydromorphone use when his mother drank herself to death, dying of cirrhosis of the liver, as his father began drinking heavier than ever.

Collectively, these students' stigma as drug addicts pained me as much as the potential damage induced by substance misuse. Drug addiction and incarceration carry similar consequences for both males and females. However, women face an ever-greater degree of terrible stigma because of gender-based stereotypes that hold women to different standards (Olphen, 3-4). Regardless, a drug-based stigma limits people's options for access to health care, drug treatment, successful employment, or stable housing (Olphen, 4). The vibe had changed to a darker shade of the grayscale.

Two big burly cops quickly and stealthily barged violently into the lounge area, breaking paintings off the walls and scaring off the jazz ensemble, which dispersed like cockroaches burrowing into molehills. It appeared some of the cops understood the concept of hitting the gym instead of the donut fix fairy. A cop barked, "All right, the jig is up. We know that you have violated probation for dealing cocaine and possession of narcotics with intent to distribute. You are going away for a long time. Put your hands behind your back and walk outside peacefully and we won't kill you in the street like the filthy cokehead scum you are, and bag ourselves another extra paycheck." He immediately bolted from the basement in a state of panic, as he still was carrying coke on him but became soon tackled by one police officer. The man displayed impressive form, pinning him down in a full-body tackle as a bag of cocaine fell out of his pocket. As they carted him off to jail, the other cop surreptitiously helped himself to a dropped bag of cocaine in front of the partygoers and snorted it himself in a nearby bathroom. This cop's nose was heavily chalked up with white powder as my mouth fell to the floor in shock as my bloodshot eyes seemed to pop right out of my skull in horror. No one noticed the coked-up law officer or his pinned pupils, as nearly everyone was dead wasted and soon the students passed out; they were so drunk they seemed to be comatose. All were knocked out except for me. I fought in vain to hold on to my damaged body and my crippled, tormented mind. I was still reeling from witnessing the arrest when I knocked on the grad student's door. There was no reply, so I opened the door, and the graduate student was staring back at me, pale, white as a ghost. Two hydromorphone syringes lodged deep within his arms. I could not stop crying or puking for the next twenty minutes. He had overdosed on a combination of hydromorphone and valium, and while the cops were busy dealing with the drug dealers, another bright young adult mind was extinguished in active addiction. It became abundantly clear to me that society could not arrest its way out of addiction.

Seeing so many brilliant young minds fall prey to extreme substance abuse was a situation I would wish on absolutely no one! Little did I realize I would eventually surpass the using rates of most practicing addicts in college yet somehow survive. I walked back to my dorm room alone, coming down from the weed, knowing that my innocence might never return. My heart had hardened due to the severity and weight of what I had experienced. You do not see people smoking crack in public with no consequences and ever go back to a normal lifestyle. While my Cannabis smoking was not an everyday habit during my first two years of using, but it quickly became more and more psychologically habitual, especially after I added my regularly drinking alcohol. After the first two years of experimenting, Marijuana became my antidote to the adverse effects of my overconsumption of alcohol, not to mention my remedy for everything else in life. It honestly became more than an addiction but an entire way of life until 2020, when I finally, God-willing, kicked marijuana for good. I had started pre-gaming with fat bong rips and smoking endless joints instead of beer. This was a natural transition. When I could not find Cannabis, my alcohol consumption went through the roof. There was not enough vodka in the capital of Moscow to satiate my ravenous cravings—averaging five to ten shots every weekend; urinating on any public property I could find and puking wherever I pleased. I was beyond fucked up; I was a new dictionary definition of loaded that has not been defined yet! I was a walking time bomb of self-destruction, ready to explode at a moment's notice! My hangovers were becoming worse and worse. Although I never fell behind in my studies, my social life deteriorated to hanging out solely with people who abused drugs and alcohol as I did. My genuine friends began alienating themselves from me because they had no interest in watching me self-destruct on such an extreme level. It was sordid and so sad, and I remained so lost in my forest of delusion that I did not see any dilemmas, even when my addiction was staring me directly in the face. By the end of my substance misuse, I lost my creativity, friends, self-respect, pride, and most of my money. Without self-control, drugs will destroy your memory, your self-respect, and everything that goes along with your self-esteem. Addiction will eventually show you a gruesome living hell that I would not wish on anyone in the world!

I eventually left my college, performing what is known in the business as a geographic treatment that never works no matter the person's intentions. The drugs, my demons, my character defects and my drug connections followed me everywhere I went, as did my unresolved trauma, PTSD, and need to escape from those demons using other monsters! It would take many, **MANY** more years of wretched self-abuse to counter my destructive habits with deep self-reflection and self-acceptance and to embrace a clean and far more respectful way of life. Unable to shake my burgeoning PTSD had reduced my social functioning to rock-bottom levels. My self-medication with alcohol and drugs only exacerbated my social and cognitive dissonances. I became aloof, separating myself from everyone around me in between hits. I used in excess enough that eventually withdrawals and undesirable side effects followed me around even when not using. I was too drunk and high constantly to understand why this was happening. Due to my traumatized and twisted view of the universe, sobriety was a cruel joke of nature devised to highlight all my insecurities and fears, all of which dissolved like magic after the first hit or sip.

I did not realize that people who engage in any pleasurable activity with temperance and/or moderation successfully know their limits enough not to experience withdrawals when they alter the behavior and are self-actualized enough inside their hearts and souls; they prefer variety in all their daily activities to avoid burnout or boredom. They also prioritize achieving goals systematically and incrementally as a central focus in their lives before engaging in pleasurable activities, deriving joy through nurturing their responsibilities. A crucial and critical difference between healthy individuals and addicts who self-destruct is that addicts obsess over external pressures to control their addictions, so they do not have to stop, ignoring the need to reduce or abstain to achieve an enjoyable balanced life. Healthy individuals (because of being self-actualized and self-disciplined) engage in behaviors moderately) with no effort or thought each time, naturally, because their life goals and ambitions matter far more to them than short-term pleasure at the expense of their long-term happiness. I could only quit drugs for good and turn my life around when I recognized this mindset. That was the critical moment when I begrudgingly admitted to myself that I will always have the all-or-nothing addict mindset for nearly every activity I do, good and bad. If I did not have a problem with drugs, I would not obsessively think about the same topic every minute of the day, despite all the damage I eventually did to myself. Until I recognized this mindset, sobriety was impossible to embrace, and I could not change my destructive behaviors! Denial and any addictions are husband and wife. They go hand in hand.

I will never achieve this balance with drugs. I have lied through my teeth to myself about balance constantly to avoid the naturally discomforting process of facing both my addiction and my traumas aggravated through active addiction. This is all an active addict is concerned about, only themselves and staying high at all costs! It is easier to keep drinking and using drugs then to face yourself as you are. This attitude extends far beyond drugs for people, to any activity we become accustomed to as a coping mechanism makes us selfish, neglectful, and self-destructive. After my first two years of responsible drug use, I consciously decided to make drugs a way of life and become a drug addict. Being an addict to me was always my choice. I do not buy the powerlessness 12-Step disease model and never will. Instead, I believe powerlessness over drug use or life events is a self-fulfilling prophecy. Addict's use learned helplessness to justify staying loaded and institutions use learned helplessness to shame and control financial, sociocultural, and spiritual assets of weaker individuals. That is just a scapegoat that the rehabilitation centers use to bleed money from the gullible and weak-minded. Never again will I buy into the same trap of learned helplessness!

Addiction is a choice people make shaped by their internal and external environments, as proven by the Rat Park experiment (Hari, 2015). This experiment involved two sets of rats. One set was placed in isolated cages where all they could do was dose themselves with morphine and cocaine, and the rats dosed themselves with dope until they died. The other set of rats were placed in a large open space designed to be heaven for rats. They were provided with lots of cheese, toys, natural elements and other rats to socialize with, as well as easy access to the same drugs. Several rats that had already habituated to morphine and cocaine were taken out of the isolation cages and placed in Rat Park, where they either rarely took the drugs or avoided them altogether, even when the scientists added sugar to the morphine and cocaine to bait the addicted rats (Hari, 2015)!

My priority used to be getting high and staying as high as possible, to such an insane degree that I overlooked the life shattering withdrawal side effects that were messing up my sober life to justify continuing getting loaded. My withdrawals became worse overtime and that would never have happened if I did not make drug-taking a daily to semi-daily routine! I had no remorse; drugs were now the very oxygen I needed to breathe. Being a drug addict was my way of coping with a world and a trauma I found unbearable. I routinely stole liquor from my parent's liquor cabinet, downing fifths of vodka and chasing it with Four Loko every weekend. These rituals became blackout drinking patterns every night until I went completely insane. I drank myself to sleep every night and got the shakes all day without alcohol, making me an antisocial maniac unless severely under the influence. The only way I could communicate pleasantly with my parents (not to mention anyone else) was when high or drunk, so I began smoking Marijuana all the time, experimenting with other drugs and drinking myself into a stupor daily. This increase in my drugging was effortless and assisted me to rationalize my deteriorating self-esteem. While I was able to maintain a high GPA, I had zero discipline outside of my writing and creative pursuits or life skills and my social life vanished. That did not matter to me at the time, it left more time for self-pity and escapism.

I no longer cared about going out with friends or pursuing new interests or hobbies but would rather sit in my room high and drunk, writing and painting for hours, while listening to reggae beats and hip-hop jams. I did not realize that my overreliance on self-medicating was seriously stunting my personal growth, nor did I care to give a fuck because the feeling of being high was far too good to resist. Sobriety had become unendurable because I preferred to numb myself instead of developing a constructive use for my boredom, which is my single greatest regret about my drug misuse, because it handicapped me and shut down plentiful opportunities for most of my twenties. Being a drug addict was not self-destructive in my traumatized mindset. It was an identity I could call my own, strength to allow myself to rise in a cruel world I could not understand, endure, or comprehend. It gave me a sense of purpose, albeit a self-destructive and delusional one. Having a purpose is the antidote to boredom and self-destructive behaviors. It is the fuel that fires the flame of all motivation, which makes life worth living.

When I left college, I rationalized the move to get away from the drugs, but when you are an addict, the drugs always find you. I found a local drug dealer by my art school, and he would sell me 4-gram eighths where the marijuana was twice as potent as anything I smoked in college, getting me twice as high smoking half the pot. I was in pothead heaven!

The trouble was, although I did not realize it, I was getting ripped off. The dispensaries sell the more potent product at a lower price than the local black market. When it was not possible to get Cannabis, which was a rare occasion, being in the pot-drenched sunny state of California I drank myself into a state of absolute wasted oblivion. In retrospect, I was not physically addicted to marijuana initially, as there is little to no physical addiction. Still, I had an eight-and-a-half-year period of total mental dependency on Cannabis. By the time I quit smoking weed for good, I experienced unpleasant physical withdrawal symptoms. This was nothing remotely like the living nightmare of opiate withdrawal, but still awful. However, my mental dependency on pot was infinitely greater because of the strongly ingrained, false belief that I needed to smoke cannabis excessively to realize my full creative potential as a writer. This seems ironic to me now, because after my first two years of smoking marijuana, Kush went from enhancing my creativity to numbing it nearly out in the end. Once I finally quit smoking Cannabis constantly, my writing and artistic abilities strengthened to the next level; these evolved even further once I entirely, God-willing, quit pot.

My 12 Step sponsors called me a fuckup. Although I failed four rehabs and four sober livings, I graduated in the top 1% of a highly regarded online university, despite being a full-blown pothead and, unfortunately, decaying active garbage bin for narcotics. Sadly, my dark aura and delusional attitude was: "Fuck him, he was always wrong. Being an addict and a dope fiend is great for me. Smoking ounces of weed every day is harmless! Opiates make me feel the happiness and security that people will never give me for the rest of my life. Reality is horrible, and I will stay loaded every single day until I die!" Cannabis, at one point, became the difference between life and death, reinforcing my destructive beliefs. The only tool that enabled me to survive a hellish cold turkey opiate kicks the first three months off a severe opiate addiction that nearly cost me my life from 2016 to 2017. Sometimes I wish I could go back in time and deck my old self while Falcon kicking myself in the balls for my delusional, destructive insanity and the horrible pain I put my loved ones through. Since I cannot change the past, I pray to God for repentance and redemption in living out the rest of my days clean and sober.

CHAPTER 8

OFF THE RAILS

THE ULTIMATE IRONY IS THAT DAILY CANNABIS SMOKING WOULD TURN on me from 2017 to 2020 despite freeing myself from opiates that same year. Marijuana had once deeply inspired and enhanced my creativity when I only used it twice per week. Through my billowing weed fog, I finally realized that my daily marijuana abuse (not to mention more than a liberal intake of other drugs) was dramatically inhibiting, nay destroying my creative impulses. In contrast, they aided the creative process at first and burned me out severely, leaving me paranoid, apathetic, and deeply depressed. My tolerance became so insane that no matter how much I smoked, the Cannabis high was a shadow of its former absolute glory, and this was no one's fault but my own. I denied it for as long as I could until at last on the fateful day, I realized that despite my appreciation for Cannabis, the stoner lifestyle was making me utterly miserable. Cannabis when utilized properly has powerful life changing experiences to bestow, but my gluttony and excessive pot use had intensified my self-loathing and began fragmenting my sense of self to an unbearable level, because I could no longer control my consumption. Cannabis controlled me and marijuana made all my decisions for me. It was time for a permanent change. That realization was the Jenga block that toppled my Jenga tower and ended my Cannabis abuse for good—God willing! My current practice is sobriety and extreme temperance in all virtues and vices, and I refuse to change that for anything! The greatest irony that I have learned is that less often I smoked Cannabis, the more rewarding the experience was! The Cannabis plant has taught me the utmost importance of self-control in all my affairs from henceforth until I die. Because I cannot use drugs moderately or temperately in the long-term, I always prefer to abuse them in the end, and they always end up taking over my life (and I tried countless times desperately to achieve that balance before finally surrendering to recovery)! I know the best path for me today is absolute abstinence! Honestly will always, to a degree, love drugs as much as I hate them. Frankly, the reason I am sober today is that I realized I loved drugs so much that I willingly let them ruin my life, mind, body, and soul, a complete package of self-destruction mentally, psychically, and spiritually. I never want to be the selfish, broken, and self-destructive strung-out nightmare I once was. I would not wish the last few years of my addiction to my very worst enemy or the murderer of my entire family.

The moral is to stay sober. Otherwise, be responsible and temperate in all your drug consumption or any pleasurable activities that have the potential for addiction. Or watch your life & your goals dismantle right out from under you! *The War on Drugs* is immoral and must end because drugs remain unfairly scapegoated as the cause of addiction when anything and everything can become a self-destructive addiction. Even positive activities in and of themselves can become destructive without self-control. Balance, self-discipline, and variety are everything in life! I loved the effects of mind-altering chemicals so much that I willingly crossed that line into addiction and could never use them in moderation/temperance from the age of 21 onward. I also developed a crippling insistence on sameness in my activities that extended far beyond drugs to hide from childhood trauma. Then the drugs became my only priority, and everything else fell by the wayside, as it is for every active drug addict. All my loved ones and friends become secondary to my using buddies and using activities. It was more than an addiction to me; It was my entire way of life and my subcultural social network. Once we relapse, unlike ordinary people who take drugs recreationally, it becomes our sole priority. We are willing, unlike non-addicts, to throw our morality out the window to get what we want, no matter what the cost.

———————◗———————

One hit of weed is not enough for me, and neither is a billion hits of weed, no matter how long I stay sober! The 800-pound gorilla only hibernates, and if he wakes up, he is always hungrier than the last insanity merry-go-round. If I foolishly wake him up again, he will never go back into stasis, and I will have nothing left but emptiness. Whenever I controlled my drug use, I felt like I was eating 1/10th of an entire steak & egg dinner with no seasoning. Whenever I thoroughly enjoyed my drug use, there was no attempt at control. Ordinary people seldom or ever have this issue with psychoactive chemicals or pleasurable activities, and I admittedly envy them. Moderation/temperance, unlike for others, is living torture. Trying to use my drugs of choice in moderation or self-disciplined is like eating 1/10th of a tiramisu cake then watching everyone else eat the rest of the cake in front of me while drinking champagne as my mouth falls off my face! It is a seething volcano waiting to implode! I cannot expect anything but permanent misery if I compromise myself. After quitting alcohol, I became deliberately forced to look at my Cannabis and drug abuse and take an authentic look at the reasons behind my daily pot-smoking—boredom and fear of lacking creative purpose and vision for my career. In recovery, boredom and the necessity of purpose sit alongside HALT for addicts, and every individual has different needs to alleviate boredom in recovery to find meaning and happiness. Happiness never comes cheap; It is the most expensively gained emotion on the planet, requiring self-discipline and a concentrated will to reap the tremendous benefits and rewards. It is not enough for schools to push the D.A.R.E agenda of "drugs are dangerous." We must teach our children why self-discipline and self-control matter in this world, why time & money management are so invaluable as assets. We must also teach our children that anything can become an addiction that will destroy your lifestyle, even virtuous activities taken to extremes.

I used Cannabis temperately for the first two years of smoking weed before it became a psychological daily to semi-daily habit. It would take another five years of chronic pot smoking before I began getting brain fog and impairing withdrawal symptoms. **NEVER** become a pothead/stoner like I used to be, as you will eventually regret all the time and money that disappeared without you caring because you became too burned out on the herb even to notice.

I support the legalization of all drugs and the end of *The War on Drugs*. However, I will admit that marijuana with a high tolerance and daily toking has the potential more than any other drug for completely screwing up your life. In such a sneaky, subtle fashion, you will not notice it! I know because I was a massive pothead throughout my twenties, but I never saw the problem until ten years later. This happens because a high tolerance of Cannabis impairs, even destroys, creativity and social skills as it eventually makes you FAR too comfortable with boredom and therefore, too satisfied with complacency and stagnation. Ultimately, this robs you of what you could become unless you either quit entirely or dramatically reduce your consumption for the rest of your life. However, for addicts the second option is impossible to achieve in the long-term. Unless an addict can honestly admit this to themselves, all is lost. This goes for all drugs, not just pot. Still, because pot's negatives are so subtle compared to other drugs, it takes far longer to realize that there is a problem with addictive use, making it not physically, but psychologically more dangerous.

I quit entirely because moderation/temperance for me is near impossible, as even with a high tolerance I came to realize that I still liked the effects of the drugs far too much. I always wanted to both achieve all my goals and dreams while I stayed loaded. Yet, if push came to shove, and any opportunities or dreams required me to sacrifice getting loaded, anything else was expendable to me. I cannot even begin to count the number of false starts to sobriety or extreme temperance I had always with the greatest reservations imaginable where I convinced myself, "This time will be different. This time I will learn to moderate my drug use for good! I'm sure as fuck not quitting the sacred herb or my beloved liquor and Oxy forever." I was not interested in cleaning up or changing my lifestyle until 2020, when I'd lost a decade of my life. Even after realizing that at twenty-nine I was a pathetic burnt-out shell of everything I once was at twenty-one, getting loaded was too important to me to imagine a life without drinking and using drugs. The feeling of invulnerability to others' criticism and numbness to the fear of failure meant I did not care about my own defects or failings enough, so that getting loaded was both addictive and attractive. I was interested in learning how to have my cake and eat it too, nothing else. Had I continued practicing rare drug consumption, I could have had this wish, but my greed, selfishness, and lack of self-control destroyed that dream as I lost any sense of self-agency. My periods of clean time in 2018 shrank as my drug binges increased. That diseased thinking that getting loaded was giving me something of worth enough to sacrifice my true values cut me off from everything and everyone I cared about in my life. Inevitably, I would always start the cycle of substance abuse again and again, leaving myself more dead than alive. God-willing, I refuse to take the bait ever again.

The War on Drugs is immoral because its scapegoats' drugs as the cause of addictive behavior when the mindset is the true culprit. We live in a modern society that promotes addiction and impulse at every opportunity. I had avoided drinking excessively with my girlfriend at first. Still, when I learned, she was cheating on me with six other guys, Sunk into a disgusting, self-pitying, catatonic well of hopeless despair. I quickly lost all control and could not stop binge drinking liquor. I noticed that I could have some modicum managing how much Cannabis became smoked (the regime I eventually lost in 2018 and 2019). Still, when drunk on alcohol, self-control became outright impossible, and I would binge on both into absolute oblivion. Now my life revolved around a continuous supply of weed and alcohol, for without them by this time, I could not function at all! Some people's lives fall apart because, under the influence of drugs, they lose all their creativity and motivation. They do not tell you about the people who experience the 10,000% worse outcome. Being useless when sober and solely creative, motivated, and able to function at mere baseline **ONLY WHEN UNDER THE INFLUENCE OF DRUGS!!!** Sadly, from 2018 to 2020, by the end of my drug career that had become my life. And eventually, the drugs stopped working for me to influence anything productive or creative because my tolerance was too high to get those benefits without spending a fortune and destroying myself chasing the nearly unattainable virgin high at this point. Smoking chronic blunts for breakfast, drinking beer, popping Valium chased down with lean for lunch, fifths of vodka, and OxyContin for dinner as my lunatic psychosis routine. Not that the other drugs mattered anymore, OxyContin and Opana were the very air that I breathed, the only spiritual nourishment I required times 10,000% and then some!

Grab the serenity, the happiness, and fulfillment of scoring a Superbowl winning touchdown! Racks of lamb, twilight bathing in a hot tub made of gold and Belgian chocolate fudge, with champagne overflowing with holy water by the bedside! Combine the joy and security from earning enough money to become a millionaire or a billionaire. Experience the spiritual enlightenment of mastering the art of guided meditation, donating to a just or noble cause, discovering new science, or curing a life-threatening disease that poisoned the souls of millions of people. Use the excitement of finding a new planet, contacting alien life-forms who shared the wisdom of the galaxy, and advanced humanity thousands of years in a single convention. Multiply that pleasure by 500,000%, and you are still **nowhere** close to the experience of opiates. Not even in the same league. Nothing as genuinely evil as opiates has **any** right to exist in this world. They are the only class of drugs where most will **beg** to sell their soul, just for a taste of the supreme artificial heaven they provide, above and beyond any earthly description. The pleasures of opiates exist despite the living hell of the dreaded junk kick! The only drug where you could lose everyone and everything you ever loved in your existence and simply shrug it off. The feeling from a perfectly calculated dose of opiates is stronger than any emotion on Earth, more powerful a sensation than anyone should ever experience, and for better and for much worse you're never the same after tasting literal artificial paradise.

Utter nothingness, the supreme apathy. More opiates will always solve that problem, the great panacea of the human condition of pain, yet bring pain such as no soul should ever dare to feel! Most people consider the speedball (Heroin & Cocaine) the pinnacle of the devil's temptations surely designated to bring humankind to their knees. I am afraid I must disagree. For me, the ultimate high and my greatest weakness is the dreaded but incredible Canna-poppy (the combination of Cannabis and opiates)! The high lasts a good eleven to twelve hours. Opiates are euphoric enough on their own but combined with potent Cannabis the euphoria is disturbingly unmatched by anything in this world! Codeine & OxyCodone with dab-soaked Kush makes me so euphoric I could watch all my loved ones die with no pain, suffering, emotions, or sorrow. That nirvana feeling is all that matters. Values and morals I could have spent an entire lifetime developing into a lifestyle that will become unceremoniously purged from my existence. The one critical difference between a regular drug addict and a dope fiend is that even the worst drug addicts keep a semblance of their base humanity and principles or attempt to keep these elements intact for as long as the facade of functionality serves them. A dope fiend does not need society when junk provides a penultimate euphoria that nothing on this planet could ever match, only matched by the hellish living insanity of junk sickness. When the addict finds his or her drug of choice, the trap door does not shut on them. We willingly shut the trap door and swallow the key on ourselves. At that moment, no life experience could give us what we want or need more than that bag of drugs or behavior does so effectively. We become willing to subjugate ourselves to a systematic dismantling of our baseline humanity to maintain the euphoria by any means necessary. Lying, stealing, cheating, and conning become as natural as breathing. But the higher you go into heaven…, the lower you must fall into hell. To most true addicts, the hell on Earth is worth enduring for a taste of chemical heaven and bliss without effort! Happiness without investment to any individual with unresolved trauma, having failed to achieve the joys of self-actualization is utterly priceless. Morals become immaterial to relief, more than the cyclical pain of pleasure itself.

———————●———————

Nothing is emptier than the synthetic bliss of the opiate high, for pleasure of such magnitude is always, inevitably followed by absolute misery. You honestly believe that you will never know happiness again without chemical subjugation. My alcohol, Cannabis, psychedelics, and above all, my opiate consumption became so extreme that I began avoiding food and even water to get more drunk, more stoned, trip harder, and nod harder, withering away in mental and physical decay. The nod is the state that all opiate users desire to reach in the high; a blissful state between waking and sleep where you can control your dreams in real time as you get the best sleep of your life, yet you can wake up at any moment. Artificially, I felt happier than I had ever felt in my existence or had any right to feel. I knew that my addiction was letting me exist at a fraction of my true potential, sedating and numbing my creative faculties and pushing my loved ones and friends away from me as I willingly self-destructed. Yet I remained in this state quite willingly until my family and I discovered effective childhood trauma treatment in 2020. Far too often according to Smith's (2016) research and the DSM-5 (APA, 2013) model for addiction treatment, substance use disorder and the problems in an individual's life are narrowed down to the drugs themselves as the problem, rather than the childhood traumas that make habitual self-medicating so attractive in the first place. In my experience, the drugs are never the problem. The underlying unresolved traumatic garbage a person experienced is the true culprit. The 12-Step program mostly exacerbated my addictive tendencies to increasingly extreme levels of self-abuse until the underlying childhood trauma was effectively healed. I did the 12 steps multiple times before the correct treatment, but they made it impossible for me to forgive myself or move on from my past into a clean lifestyle because the underlying wounds were never addressed. I have had a far better experience with my last two AA sponsors. However, sometimes, I find the 12-Step model dogmatic. I've experienced the ways in which this model can be narrow-minded, while focusing too much on the negatives of self. AA offers very little that leads to self-actualization or how to build yourself up into something greater than your past. Instead, without the ability to correctly process my childhood trauma into constructive energy, the 12-Step program caused my self-loathing to mushroom, which increased my need to escape the world. The past in most rehabilitation centers is constantly bludgeoned into your face like a hammer—shame and fear are utilized as the sustaining motivators for change in addicts. But fear and self-loathing are normal states to an addict, and seldom create positive changes in people. Often these emotions aggravate the addictive behaviors they attempt to correct. My poor mother spent one night holding my head above the bowl after I polished off my half-eaten meal with endless bottles of vodka and tequila to drown out the knowledge of my girlfriend's infidelity. When my parents attempted to curb my all-encompassing addictions and began drug testing me for marijuana, I started smoking radioactive fertilizer, flowers and grass by the handful from random lawns without a second's hesitation as my drinking spiraled further out of control, while my skin turned to leather in response. No joke. I went out trolling the property of random neighbors and picked handfuls of any random flower patch I could find, put it in my bowl, and smoked it.

My drinking was totally out of control by 2012, wasted nightly and religiously. I do not know how I maintained such a high GPA and was called a superhuman academic genius during the worst of my binges. I did it all seamlessly while loaded, tripping balls, and utterly smoked out of my mind! The combination of productivity and heavy drug intake lasted only two years before my destructive habits began inhibiting my creativity and goals. And by the third year, I started a true religion of denial that the drugs no longer worked as they did initially because of my lack of self-control. Smoking fertilized grass gave me a strange buzz which made me believe it was working as a "substitute." Accordingly, I began smoking toxic grass and flower patches regularly to make up for not being able to smoke weed, chasing it down with liquor. It was pure delusion and utter psychotic insanity. When my parents discovered a vast supply of fertilizer laced grass and weeds, packaged in individual baggies along with an assortment of flowers, in horror, they offered me natural Cannabis to get me to stop smoking whatever I found on neighbors' lawns, which worked like a charm! Unfortunately, every other aspect of my life was in a downward spiral phase. I would stop using occasionally for all my classes. Still, I eventually realized I was too depressed and dysfunctional sober to give a shit about my schoolwork or my life as I once did, and I snapped back to the drugs like a rubber band. I was getting high from the moment I woke up to the moment I went to sleep seven days a week like clockwork and drinking myself into drunken blackout oblivion every single night. I was so physically dependent on alcohol by this stage that when I first attempted to detox on my own, I shook violently in pain, every nerve in my spine squirming about in a vicious pool of writhing agony. Every cell in my body craved a drink or a drug. Sleep without liquor, weed and beer combined was now physically impossible.

Naturally, I had to fortify myself with two belts of straight vodka, a quarter ounce of weed and cases of beer, stolen right out of my parent's liquor cabinet. I did not even care to refill the vodka bottles with water to disguise my tracks once the relationship with my promiscuous harlot of a girlfriend decayed. I entered this consciousness restricting world of repetition, where only one thing mattered—getting my drug and alcohol fixes. Smoking weed from the moment I woke up and blazed all day long, then getting drunk until I passed out nightly. After receiving said fix, I would feel much better about the tangled web of hopeless insanity that was now my broken life.

I thought the lifestyle of an addict was so glamorous at first, and for the first two years of using, it indeed was enchanting in the seediest, hedonistic way. That glamor quickly turned to squalor after the first two years when I stopped moderating my intake, and things never improved until I finally kicked all drugs (including marijuana) in May 2020. I drove under the influence almost regularly, and it is a veritable miracle I did not harm myself or anyone else. Many close calls occurred while driving intoxicated. I was so drunk behind the wheel three times; I was practically asleep at the red lights. One night I drank six Four Lokos back-to-back and nearly killed myself and six girls who were high on weed and cocaine, almost drove into a pole on the Hollywood streets at eighty miles per hour! Sordidly, those kinds of events were typical for me now. If it were not for the MacGyver maneuvers of my ex-coked-out girlfriend, we all would have been dead! We were all far too stoned and drunk to contemplate our narrow brush with death. I celebrated my survival by pounding cases of beer and gulping down shots of vodka into oblivion, then having sex with a five-hundred-pound whale I randomly encountered. Sex was now merely a distraction from my insane, unadulterated self-loathing. Like alcohol and drugs, sex as a form of self-medication never made me feel complete, because no love was ever involved—only lust wrapped in a clever disguise of companionship, coupled with being high together and believing the relationship had staying power only when both of us were loaded. As soon as sobriety hit, any attraction withered to nothing.

Finally, the charade that was my existence crumbled into tiny, shattered substance abused pieces because of my rampant alcohol and drug consumption. Worse still, I did not give a shit if I remained continuously intoxicated to hide from my emotions and hide from myself and my life. The drugs gave me an artificial feeling of power and control, a control that was a deceptive and destructive illusion when you come to rely on chemicals for baseline happiness. Non-addicted people can ensure that they maintain otherwise healthy lifestyles even if they indulge from time to time. Once you cross that line, it can never be uncrossed with people engaged in substance misuse because of genetic synaptic changes in the hippocampus of people who graduate from recreational drug use to full-blown drug addiction. No matter how long a substance abuser is detoxed or clean, they are always at risk of relapse. The addictive process nearly always reactivates should they relapse, which reactivates the cravings in an addicted brain from where they left off that can make cessation or moderation of intake next to impossible! People with a history of chronic drug use suffer far greater and prolonged withdrawals than temperate drug users or abstainers. I had to learn that lesson as an addict in the most brutal way possible. I did not see the point of art school having realized I should never have left pursuing my writing career in the first place. I made an enormous mistake that had cost my family thousands of dollars. My shame was now unbearable, and thus the need to self-medicate my problems grew at an extraordinary pace. The girl I was having sex with did not care about me at all. She ended up sleeping with six other men. I was so unrealistic that I thought she was loyal to me when it was the THC and the alcohol talking for me.

When I realized my relationship with this girl was doomed to failure, one night I came home stoned on pot and blacked out on five shots of vodka back-to-back. I knew the combination of my dysfunctional relationship and that insidious first drink would do me in. My dealer had temporarily run out of weed, and weed was the valve that kept my alcoholism at bay when combined. Marijuana always was (and I honestly realize that weed still is) my drug of choice over alcohol, until I discovered opiates. When I drank without the weed, pure unadulterated hell was always the result. Before my parents arranged an intervention, I had stolen most of the beer from their liquor cabinet, blacked out, and thrown a large fan into the pool; this was after nearly hitting one of my best friends with it, unintentionally.

Shortly afterwards, I was drunk and faded on a mountain of mid-grade pot at my intervention, which did not help my case any. The interventionist had an exceptionally self-righteous attitude and demeanor about him. The interventionist himself was in recovery and had this real I am better than you are, holier than thou bullshit attitude, and this made me rebellious and even more self-toxic. I even left during the middle of the intervention to drink and use more, knowing full well I was not ready to stop. After the mid-grade grass had worn off, I went on an absolutely wasted tear on vodka, flying into a sordid, drunken rampage. I threw furniture wildly, swearing like a sailor on shore leave, pissing in the swimming pool, and mostly acting like a savage, untamed wild monster. I was completely out of control! The interventionist recommended in-patient treatment. I responded by getting even more intoxicated on vodka and hopping the fence. So, after running away for half a day, with my head swimming in agony through alcohol withdrawal and an inconceivable hangover, I briefly considered living on the streets. However, I realized that I had no money and therefore no way to support my poly-drug habits. I went to rehab because I believed I had no other choice. What I know in my heart today is that there is always a choice, the choice to give up, or the choice to empower yourself. Today, I choose the latter, God-forbid never the former.

CHAPTER 9

REHAB OR RE-UP?

THE FIRST STEP WAS VISITING OUTPATIENT REHAB AND I WAS IN SUCH unfathomable denial about the life-threatening severity of my addictions that it was a profoundly worthless experience. I wish I could blame drugs and alcohol for this, but I was solely to blame because I was still broken, consumed with unresolved childhood trauma I did not want to look at, selfish and self-centered to the extreme from ages 23 to 29. As a semi-functional but active addict, I cared more about getting loaded and staying loaded than anything else, including personal development. Years of unresolved PTSD and being bullied led to my internalizing myself as a worthless and unlovable human being in my natural state. I developed a passive attitude of learned helplessness that prevented me from trying new things or expanding outside my comfort zone long before I touched any psychoactive chemicals. My attitude was that all pain was only evil, and all pleasure was only good. Therefore, hedonism was the only worthy coping mechanism to deal with reality. I believe more than anything else that this self-indulgent, self-destructive attitude was the root of all my addictions. My self-abuse allowed me to medicate my fear of failure by eventually becoming too numb to even try.

I could not fail if I did not act.

Long before I touched drugs, I used food and video games in the same addictive pattern to hide from my fear of failure and numb my emotions. My addiction to these behaviors got so bad at one point; I was obsessed with Super Smash Bros alongside my friends, stomping Goombah's, and leaping across mushrooms. I forgot to dress or bathe or eat! You are never a failure for failing or attempting an action, only a failure for not making any attempt at all! When you give up on yourself, only then are you utterly lost. True winners thrive on failure and criticism because they realize that they strengthen their craft through these elements consistently and constantly. When I embraced this crucial attitude, my life transformed for the better. No one becomes a talented musician or artist if they cannot tolerate constructive criticism of their work because they shut themselves off from change, personal growth, or socio-cultural adaptability. I stayed at the rehab for only three weeks before I was kicked out of the facility for public urination that disturbed a female resident there for sex addiction treatment. I was relocated to a sober living that was anything but sober.

Our sober living began drug testing us, but that did not stop addicts from smuggling in drugs or getting loaded. As I naturally had a stash of high-grade marijuana hidden in my room, I blazed up only a week after arriving at this sober living facility because marijuana was my oxygen. Soon I was off to outpatient hospital rehab, having failed my drug test for marijuana, and I sadly did not give one fuck. My family believed my substance abuse would end after rehabilitation. In fact, my drug abuse would only get exponentially worse because of the disturbingly favored *tough love hot-seat approach*. This approach is still pathetically in vogue today. The tough love hot-seat method enables addiction facilities to become rich, with profits of six figures or more for the misery that they inflict on countless mentally ill people. They expect this approach will reduce addiction or mental illness stigma but here is a hint, you greedy bastards.

These tough-love policies sole purposes is to do the exact opposite and feed the very addictions they purport to expel. The lessons I learned in this rehab exacerbated my need for drugs and accordingly, I had to revisit the revolving doors of treatment numerous times. The people who run these facilities make six figures in the recovery subculture by promoting self-doubt, weakness and dependency that fosters recidivism and recurring investments into the same treatment that lead to the addict coming back for more abuse. There are some people in rehabilitation that genuinely care about the welfare of addicts and the mentally ill, but not only are these few and far between, these people seldom have power or influence over drug and recovery policies. There are sober livings and rehabilitation clinics that take pride in rehabilitating the mentally ill, confronting childhood traumas and providing dignity and quality of living to those who are labelled as unworthy of neither. Take exceptional time and research to find them, as an impulsive decision can cost a life!

Drug addicts already have nonexistent self-esteem and often completely hate themselves. Breaking chronic relapsers down when most are already beaten down speeds up their maladaptive condition even if they stay sober—for too many, resulting in rock bottom or death. Those who run sober living facilities and rehabilitation clinics usually do not want jack shit to change because as soon as the addict community wakes up to the facilitator's hypocrisy and greed, sacrificing Hippocratic compassion and care for profit, those in charge are out of work for life! Almost every time I arrived at detox, the entire staff was dead set on making sure everyone labeled themselves as hopeless, forever in recovery, and a never recovered alcoholic or drug addict. If not, the patients were labeled as being in a state of denial over their incurable *disease*. I had no problem admitting to my drug addictions because I was clearly different from recreational drug users who do not end up on the street or nearly broke because they cannot go a day without getting high. However, I did not believe that I was powerless over my drug habits, nor did I label myself as being powerless. This belief that rehabs insisted on clients adopting became nothing more than a deadly self-fulfilling prophecy to me and most others. These beliefs nearly destroyed what was left of me because this strict approach made me sadly believe I was worthless, unworthy, and could never change myself.

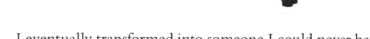

I eventually transformed into someone I could never have imagined devolving into, even in my worst living nightmare. A full-blown OxyContin and Codeine addict who smoked K2 Spice like crack cocaine, along with smoking weed daily and popping every painkiller I could get my hands on whether they were prescribed or not; all this atop of out-of-control alcoholism. Little was taught in the useless rehabilitation centers besides managing physical cravings. If anyone wanted a dual diagnosis, they were told that they were evil lying sacks of shit drug addicts in 12-Step sober livings and no other diagnosis was recognized. Underlying causes for psychological conditions were ignored or blatantly dismissed as lies from the *disease*. Tough love was favored, and as far as 60% of rehabilitation centers were concerned, all addicts were the same and deserved zero sympathy. The addiction specialists (most of whom had never taken or had any experience with drugs) had a pervasive attitude that the users had the right to either inject themselves to death or hang themselves by a noose and make society a better place by not existing. This toxic mentality pervades and still infects American institutions that deal with addiction like a terminal virus. For addicts, this is the pathetic and broken state of this country's wretched mental health care system that most often leads to recidivism. Their inhuman and malicious approach worked to neuter our valid complaints about the "medical treatment" that we were receiving, but led to plentiful chronic relapses, overdoses, suicide attempts, and countless tragic and preventable deaths.

There is an absolute difference between drug use and drug addiction, which American addiction treatment denies to the detriment of millions of vulnerable people. With responsible drug use, to which 90% of people adhere, the user always considers set and setting and does not hesitate to stay clean from alcohol and drugs when circumstances call for responsibility and sobriety (Hari, 147). In the perpetual cycle of self-flagellating addiction (no matter the addiction and not exclusive to drugs or alcohol as I have learned the hard way), the goal is escapism and getting as far away from reality as possible, no matter what the potential consequences. Someone who is addicted to reading would most likely be encouraged in this habit, but they might forget to make dinner or become so preoccupied with the book in hand that they neglect their children or other loved ones. I have made peace with my lack of self-control regarding drugs after years of steadfast denial, because I will always fall into category of excess due to my addictive nature; this will be true for me even with years or decades clean. I will never want just one, and with twenty years clean, I still will never want just one drink or just one hit! There's an invisible line that once crossed, if the user does not heed the red flags, the drug or compulsive behavior always transforms from a life accentuator into an all-consuming destroyer of life itself. For the most part, rehabilitation facilities have zero interest in keeping people sober or addiction-free, as all the money comes in making people believe they are powerless. They teach mentally ill people that relapse is a part of recovery for a simple reason; it keeps the money flowing into their pockets and our for-profit prison industries. It has nothing to do with truth or health, just greed and deception. Self-empowerment is a negative concept for most of the mental healthcare industry dealing with addiction in America, which is why I see our mental healthcare system as a self-serving evil and in dire need of a total revamp!

After three weeks of rehab, I moved to sober living, despite my adamant objection to being in a halfway house. I knew that rehab had prepared me with zero valuable tools to deal with life on life's terms. I watched people relapsing in recovery regularly, and they kicked most of them out on the streets; most of these people never made it back. I had little choice and hated myself so much that I figured nothing mattered. If I could go back in time to that moment and revisit myself, I would have said that there is always a choice. I had been barely sober for about a month when my girlfriend saw me during outpatient rehab, solely to break up with me. I did not take my first breakup with grace or fortitude. I was already emotionally vulnerable and raw, and I could once again not smoke weed being drug tested all the time, so I had nothing to distract me from my loneliness and alienation from people, not to mention a growing sense of apathy and fear about building my future.

This made the use of harder drugs I would never have touched otherwise, instantaneously appealing in the dirtiest, filthiest way possible. Since several patients were sneaking liquor into the sober living facility, I helped myself to binges of Jack Daniels, vodka, and caffeinated alcohol shots. I learned from other alcoholics and addicts how to cheat the drug tests with ease so I could drink and drug myself into sweet oblivion with reckless impunity. Despite getting caught once while drunk on a drug test and one other time for being caught with K2 Spice, it never happened again as my addiction was the focus on my thinking so much that I put forth all my efforts into staying one step ahead of random drug testing when I should have been focusing on recovery and my future. Yet, I was so utterly miserable and dysfunctional when sober, that my future was the last thing on my mind—I couldn't imagine any happy future without being loaded. Before long, I had befriended another using addict. He had no interest in being sober for any reason and so, he smuggled in bags of MDMA, blow and synthetics for everyone who did not subscribe to the program of lifetime abstinence; there were many volunteers.

At this point, convinced by AA and their "millions saved" 12 Step dogma that I was powerless over my life and powerless over my addictions, I had no interest in cutting back, making any life changes, or ever being sober for any reason at all. I felt broken and hopeless sober, consumed with self-loathing and a lack of purpose, so why stay sober, anyway? When 90% of AA meetings I attended kept drilling into our skulls continual references to what we were trying to use less of or stay away from entirely, the cure became the disease and much worse than the disease itself! I wanted to remain numbed out and stay that way.

I did not care what the consequences would be because the strict love approach convinced me that I was utterly worthless. How could I even attempt recovery on my own if I was powerless over my addiction?

I know alcoholics and drug addicts who only replace drug addiction with AA meetings as their drug of choice and never get well. Although this is not everyone in the program, those who are most grounded and centered are in the minority. According to Agent Orange, the statistical success rate of Alcoholics Anonymous despite efforts to hide any data is officially 5%, not millions of success stories (Orange, 1). At one meeting, there was a cop who was a recovered addict. He had 30 years of continuous abstinence and was unanimously voted as the most miserable human being ever. He picked fights with nearly everyone he met and got off on put downs and controlling everyone around him. It's no surprise his wife divorced him even after 30 years of recovery. However, these are genuinely good people in AA who are recovered or recovering. Rather than giving full credit to AA principles, these are hardworking and disciplined individuals who naturally practice empathy and love towards others.

My new friend and I snuck out of the sober living facility, giggling like maniac rock-star schoolgirls, and I was introduced to a drug called K2 Spice, which I was able to easily purchase at any smoke shop, at that time. I can count on one hand the times this psychotic medication from the very bottom of hell ever felt like Cannabis. Zero times. The only way to describe the K2 Spice high would be to imagine eating the brownest acid imaginable, dipped in a river of a meth lab crack, stirred up with angel dust. Psychedelics expanded implicit awareness and consciousness, and I was about to learn the ugly opposite side of the equation. Crippling physical addiction combined with psychological habituation so extreme I became an instant K2 Spice addict. K2 Spice is the black hole of despair that sucks in new souls full of vitality and life, spitting out withering husks of human beings, living solely to fix themselves a convenient overdose of death.

Most addicts stay selfish, controlling, petty, and stuck because they adopt one-size-fits all life policies. They shut out of their awareness the possibility of absorbing new information. For many of them, AA has now become the fix and more vital to them than a job, passion, or personal accountability for their sober or intoxicated actions. It is the same destructive mentality, dressed in a pretty bow with lace. So, we escaped the sober living facility, finding refuge in the dark world of synthetic drugs. Psychotic delusions and a physical addiction combined with withdrawals so extreme I became an instant K2 spice addict. I was a full-blown junkie by 27 years old, consuming 50g to 100g of pure OxyCodone and Opana, drinking two to three sixteen-ounce bottles of codeine happily per day like iced tea. My withdrawal from my junk habit, as hellish as it was, could never compare to the teeth-gnashing psychosis of synthetic drugs like K2 Spice that made me wish everyone and everything around me was dead in between hits. I experienced hot sweats like wandering in the Sahara, which transitioned to cold chills that disfigured my bones and destroyed all my will or resolve to stay clean, because the drug dug its claws into me in less than one week of experimentation. Quitting K2 Spice, I was failing miserably. My symptoms included crapping out my guts as my bones writhed in existential horror, hot sweats, icy chills, and skin-crawling tremors. I lost any pretense of morality on K2 Spice and would say and do anything for that next hopeless fix. Sleep became impossible now unless I smoked at least eight Spice blunts in a row. This unimaginable torment became only eased through hitting the spice pipe crack-head style, every ten minutes to stave off the hideous sickness. So, I spent hours every day in my sober living, and many rehabs visit fixing hard drugs for days in the bathroom. I no longer felt like a human being, and that sadly was the way I liked life now. Emotions hurt too much. I was alive, if I stayed loaded enough. I could make myself immune to the constant feelings of self-loathing and apathy that had become every single day alive.

Now I had a way out of the unbearable lack of purpose in my life that could not be tested for at the time and I did not give a fuck if it killed me because the tough love approach only amplified with each rehab, convincing me I was a worthless human being and deserved to die; so why not enjoy the ride down on the way? K2 Spice was not detectable in the drug tests until 2019. My running buddy and I were urine tested and came up clean as whistles, glorious for two selfish lunatic chronic relapsers such as ourselves. The sober living managers suspected we were using and threatened to kick us out if we did not come clean. It did not matter that we weren't caught on the urinalysis, because while smoked out of my mind, I had dropped a bag of K2 Spice in the middle of an AA meeting, and they caught us red-handed. The sober living took away my license, money, and social security card. As the straight living managers lectured me on how worthless I was for relapsing, my drug cravings got progressively worse, then became utterly unbearable. The following day, in complete K2 Spice withdrawal, and sordidly craving a hit, which I cared about by now more than my life which was now nonexistent in-between doses of dope. I had successfully manipulated the Armenian sober living manager (who shot up meth and order prostitutes inside the facilities and never got caught), into giving me back everything the manager had confiscated, which meant I was smoking K2 Spice nearly daily again.

This time I waited three days in between Spice sessions so I would always test clean and did. K2 Spice, unlike marijuana, rapidly vanishes from the urine. However, my binge drinking during the 3-day intersession period eventually led to concessions with increasing K2 Spice use. I never got caught again because the Armenian sober living manager had not only cheated on his wife but had also relapsed on crystal meth. Professional addicts had taught me tricks in rehab that allowed me to pass nearly every random drug test with flying colors, despite being fucked up out of my mind 24/7. Tweaked out of his gourd, the Armenian attempted to get my mind off drugs by driving me down to the seediest motel in the Valley, where he hired several prostitutes to give us both a blowjob. I did not give a fuck anymore because I had no job, was not in school, and had no genuine reason not to remain fucked up. Some clients at this sober living were growing pot in an underground tunnel and were selling K2 Spice and synthetic urine to halfway house clients. They were selling narcotics like hotcakes. It did not matter. When my parents learned about what was going on in this *sober* living, they transferred me to a new sober house. I brought the K2 Spice with me and smoked it in the bathroom. I had no fear of death, consequences, or the inevitable karma that was approaching, which would beat my sorry ass black and blue.

This new sober living thrived and operated through the strict love approach. I already wholly hated myself and believed I was hopeless, so this method lit the match to my gasoline tank of addiction and pulled the metaphorical trigger. AA meetings favored preaching about the evils of alcohol and the dangers of mind-altering substances while we all guzzled caffeine and chain-smoked *harmless* tobacco cigarettes to get through each day without our drugs of choice. Smoke breaks occurred with impunity. The people who ran these facilities said drugs were *bad* and how much of a gateway drug marijuana is. They also advised taking things one day at a time to quit nicotine, the single deadliest drug on the entire planet. I became addicted to smoking tobacco and eventually vaping nicotine. I smoked two to three packs of tobacco per day, chain-smoking cigarettes right down to the filters, then lighting another cigarette immediately before the first one was out. I didn't worry that this could turn my lungs blacker than a coal miners pickaxe. My nerves were shot, and my social group was primarily comprised of other smokers. I was the madman with two full cigarettes lodged behind my ears at AA meetings, bumming smokes like a filthy mooch. I wasn't working and was petrified of running out of cigarettes without the ability to use mind-altering substances as I pleased. My lungs became a toxic pool of garbage, which never happened smoking weed!

Tobacco/nicotine is innocuous according to the wisdom of dangerously broken AA logic. AA's history lacks crucial historical details about the AA founders Bill and Doctor Bob as described in the Big Book, or the Twelve and Twelve. These details were purposefully omitted, because if most AA members knew the whole truth, they would run extremely far away from thinking that AA was the only method to get or stay sober. According to Orange (2016), AA meetings do not mention that Bill Wilson only quit drinking himself to death through the excessive use of psychedelic drugs. First, he utilized a quack Belladonna cure and then he dosed himself with copious amounts of LSD on and off for the rest of his life. As well, the AA meetings never mention that Bill Wilson chain-smoked tobacco which hastened his death. Nor does the Big Book discuss how Doctor Bob, who was a disciplinarian and religious authoritarian, favored sharpening wooden paddles to ensure greater physical harm to his children. At the same time, he would sneak alcohol past his wife like a spoiled child for nearly two decades, rotating his hiding spots so that his family never discovered the volume of his alcoholic consumption. From the first sobriety date of its founders, AA's history is dishonest, as this was the day Bill Wilson gave Doctor Bob just enough alcohol to steady his nerves so that he could operate on a patient—an example of felony medical malpractice. Doctor Bob suffered no punishment or loss of his medical license. Even after Doctor Bob quit drinking, his cruel and evil behavior towards his family and others never ceased. This behavior eventually led to the suicide of two of Doctor Bob's grandchildren. One of his grandchildren murdered his own granddaughter, as he committed suicide. These events were all documented in the telling narrative of "Children of the Healer" by Sue Smith Widows (Orange, 2016).

The truth few want to confront is that most people who use and drink to excess do so not because of powerlessness or disease, but because they want to numb themselves to that level. I believe that substance misuse is a choice at the most fundamental level—a tough choice to make, but a choice, nonetheless. The disease model is profoundly disempowering and dishonest because it allows people to eliminate responsibility for their behaviors and habits. This admission robs people of self-efficacy and self-actualization. Teaching addicts that they must accept their own powerlessness over their habits only increases their dangerous habits; it never ends or controls those habits. I cannot recall one time I ever used against my will. I willingly and volitionally did what I did because I profoundly enjoyed the effects of the drugs. I wanted them so thoroughly that I would go to any lengths to get more and more in my system, and I did not care about the consequences. The escape and pleasure I got from my addiction were so powerful that I am a witness—the consequences seldom deter an addict from wanting to use more and more. The disease model robs people in recovery of taking responsibility for their own choices and their own actions. AA has used a religious and moralistic model for treating addiction since the 1930s and it has not produced favorable results. These twentieth century temperance and prohibitionists still hold an iron grip on addiction treatment. Most recovery institutions despise addicts and alcoholics, pushing fundamentalist solutions over science and research, rather than any critical thinking.

I have experienced both addicts and facilitators who look down on substance users or abusers of illegal drugs, yet promote nicotine, drink excessively, and say that marijuana and other soft drugs are worse. They are uneducated fools and blatant hypocrites. Primarily, these people are steering users towards the most harmful substances, all legal and taxable and without the same stigma. I am in no way promoting marijuana or soft drugs such as psychedelics as harmless, for they are not, but although they present their own dangers, they are far less dangerous than the legal vices. Nothing is harmless in excess, even healthy outlets and activities without variety or balance can be dangerous. I have lost all rights to alter my consciousness. I know now that pathogens such as Ayahuasca, ibogaine, psylocibin, LSD and mescaline have the profound ability to rewrite and discard our deeply seated beliefs as human beings. At times it seemed that psychedelics could become the only cure for a stagnating collective human consciousness in today's modern society. In my opinion, today most people stay trapped in their own prison of contemporary xenophobia, consumerism, banality, conformity, and ignorance. I refuse to live that way any longer. I still practice nonconformity as a sober individual today.

I was a fully committed alcoholic lunatic with a dedicated pathological death wish that frightened most drug addicts. I was a man who indeed would have drunk and drugged himself to death on alcohol and hard narcotics long ago without divine intervention. The black road I fell through was a careening downward spiral. I would have never stopped had I not experienced a complete reshuffling and restructuring of my mindset, which losing a sense of self naturally provides to those souls ready to let go of fear and shame. Set and setting don't just matter when talking about drugs and alcohol, but in every single action we undertake as human beings. If you view two people, both smoking weed and drinking beer the context of set and setting matters to the result of their drinking and using. One is celebrating after getting a promotion in his preferred career. He is in a stable, happy relationship. The other person is drinking beer and smoking weed to self-medicate for the pain of both a breakup and getting fired from their job. Who is in greater danger of addiction? The answer is naturally, the second user. Again, set refers to our mindset, our ego, and how we nourish our beliefs about ourselves, while setting is the locations and people, we surround ourselves with who influence our behaviors. The person with a healthy self-image has consistent self-control. Even if he uses drugs or drinks alcohol, it is only in a place where they have the most excellent self-discipline—avoiding excessive or compulsive patterns. They will have a consistently better lifestyle than the person using drugs or alcohol to suppress unwanted emotions or feelings. This same principle applies to every behavior across the socioeconomic human spectrum, and this is equally true for women as well as men. We can eat food, play video games, make love, gamble, practice religion, even work in addictive and destructive ways when we lose sight of our emotions and the rationalizations behind how we invest in our time and actions.

The War on Drugs foolishly blames drugs and alcohol for addiction, while utterly ignoring the millions of other habits that can destroy your life—with no narcotics necessary!

I believe that passion, purpose, and addiction closely correlate, as they all require the same obsessive energy, fully realized validity and spiritual purpose. Yet without balance or self-discipline, harmony and quality of action becomes vastly compromised and is replaced by compulsion and impulsivity. I had to learn this hard lesson through the harshest, darkest path imaginable. Purpose and passion are positive addictions, rather than the excessive indulgence in vices, which ultimately takes more than vices give. Try telling that to someone who is loaded. Not a pleasant conversation! I feel that it was worth every step of the harrowing journey to become sober, for there is joy in my heart and soul once again! Setting refers to the people we surround ourselves with and our environment. If our environment is healthy and full of positive choices and people, our behavior matches this ideal. Our behavior deteriorates when the environment is destructive, superficial to our values or fake.

In addition, while Morphine sulfate, Fentanyl, Opana (Oxymorphone) and Hydromorphone (Dilaudid) are over 50 to 100 times stronger than Heroin, they carry none of the same stigmas as smack and remain substances that are legal for consumption. In fact, Heroin contains so many adulterants, it is less addictive than the legal opiates which deliver the full form of the drug but is clearly no less dangerous. This fact defies logic, science, and progress. This is how the broken American drug policy operates because *The War on Drugs* has nothing to do with keeping people healthy or self-empowered. It has everything to do with keeping the private prison industries flourishing and enabling corrupt mental health facilities to rake in cash from desperate addicts and families. They are all sold lies to turn a profit smeared in innocent blood (Hari, 2015).

Powerlessness and learned helplessness are big business creators. I have observed that when institution after institution convinces an alcoholic, a mentally ill individual, or a drug addict that they are powerless to change themselves without either divine intervention or guidance from power tripping, egomaniacal treatment counselors, the cycle continues forever. When addiction counselors make a living by bullying the mentally ill full time, the results are abysmal and unsurprising to anyone with a functional brain cell. Not that I excuse my track record of unrepentant, self-destructive, and utterly glorious fuckups in these facilities. I was so lost in servicing my addictions that I did not believe I could change anything at all. Counselors constantly drilled into my head that I must admit my powerlessness over my behavior and the running of my life (which made it extremely easy to stay loaded sunrise to sunset 24/7).

When the rehab wardens and supervisors attempted to take my cigarettes away, I responded like a petulantly sick child of Hades, sneaking hits off filthy cigarette buts in the lock-down rehab bathrooms. It was degrading and disgusting, but chronic addiction makes you do despicable actions against your genuine nature. These sober livings punished addicts by making them write tens of thousands of words by hand or do chores all day. Writing is my single greatest passion alongside music, and one of the few reasons I continue to breathe. So, this approach accomplished absolutely nothing. The demons inside my head told my drowning, delusional and deteriorating mentality, "Fuck it all. Screw everyone and everything! Fuck the entire world! Do whatever you want, all the time, and fuck the consequences. Nihilism is the only reality that allows me to survive. I want to wither away, overdose, and die. My lifestyle will get no better because they say I am powerless, and the prophecies of powerlessness are reasonable given my ugly track record. So why bother to change anything if I'm going to end up loaded again? It's always better to burn out than to fade away!" My consciousness had narrowed into a dark vortex of self-loathing. Self-medicating with drugs had become the only option short of suicide. It would only get darker for several more years until I realized where I was headed and dug myself out.

CHAPTER 10
ONE-SIZE-FITS-NO-ONE

MOST OF MY EARLY SOBER LIVING MEETINGS WERE COMPRISED OF regular tough love sessions. They would sit a drug addict in the center of the room and mercilessly bully him or her for hours until the user burst into tears or jumped aboard the ever-expanding relapse and overdose wagons. I was the prime offender, having continued my K2 spice use unabated, drinking to alcoholic blackout whenever I could not get my hands on dope. The staff's regular therapeutic sessions consisted of labeling me with such dignified titles as "Apathetic druggie lunatic, psycho degenerate filth, wet-brained nihilist rummy, a lying bag of excrement, and the absolute scum of the earth. Do you enjoy your career as Satan full-time? You are a useless piece of dog-shit garbage. Make way for the winners who legitimately try, you're a strung-out dope-fiend." I cheerfully responded to this standardized brutal love treatment with constant chronic relapses on K2 Spice. In addition, I was always tempted to mix hard liquor and painkillers with my K2 Spice in my attempt to overdose and nuke myself off the planet permanently. All the strict love approach ever did for me was to make me happier and happier to be a drug addict and desire more incredible and longer escapes from reality—nothing else. In my experience, most patients share this unfortunate reality. Still, the rehab industry will never admit wrongdoing or change this disgusting system because their corrupt system gives them six-figure profits every year when relapsed addicts engage in the revolving door syndrome nightmare! There are infinitely greater profit margins in the American mental healthcare system from people staying sick and experiencing humiliating chronic recidivism over getting and staying well. It also plays into the toxic recovery subcultural belief that some addicts must "hit bottom" before healing can occur. Many addicts die before that process begins because of this attitude.

At this point, I sadly wanted the pain I was in, living as a hopeless drug addict. I felt as if my life would forever vacillate between using for synthetic baseline contentment and trying not to use while feeling miserable! I did not care anymore because, at the time, I hated myself and wanted to die. I was listless and miserable on the drugs, but numb and falsely euphoric enough to not care about how I felt inside, which I mistook for happiness. I craved that black aura and self-destructive image to match this hopeless environment filled with burnouts who simply didn't care about life sober or loaded, and this energy was horribly contagious. I had the cliched appearance of a 90s rock star, a self-destructive dope-fiend who still pulled A's and B's in all his classes. I wanted to become the counterculture icon of the 21st century and beyond. Someone who fulfilled all the druggy stereotypes, but succeeded in his life endeavors. I pulled this off for the first five years of using and then it became impossible as the drugs became the goal much more than life itself. I had yet to take opiates at this scary moment in my life, but that rock bottom was coming soon enough. No excess was excessive enough for me. To my credit, I cultivated this image, graduating in the top 1% of my university, all while hideously strung out on a Kurt Cobain level of alcohol and drugs. Despite achieving the fantasy of functionality, this came with harrowing sacrifices and nearly lost both my life and clear sight of the man I am today; inside of my heart and soul was nothing but a liar and a thief. I had become a person who had no problem preaching responsibility to others but using up people he loved for everything he could get. Less than six months after graduating, my excessive drug consumption turned on me and rapidly built a solid iron wall on my sociability, creativity, goals, and passions, that I sordidly refused to acknowledge until I kicked my drug habits once and for all. Enough drugs were never enough for me. I always wanted more drugs no matter the cost, even though I knew drugs were unraveling me at the seams.

I was not the only casualty. I have seen that most of the addicts and alcoholics treated in the rehabs I have experienced became despondent and got exponentially worse, whether these patients stayed sober—without treating the underlying cause of their addiction—or they relapsed. 12-Step culture often encouraged everyone to practice learned helplessness in all their affairs and thought nothing of the damage this philosophy caused to society and their patients. This program promotes a self-destructive, victim mentality. The stepper begs God to change them, instead of changing themselves, because of a heavily ingrained pressure on recovering addicts to admit personal powerlessness, not just over drugs and alcohol, but in every single facet of living life. The 3rd, 6th and 7th steps essentially are begging God to do the heavy lifting for you. If God feels like doing something else, your program is in jeopardy. The spiritual axiom, "The Lord, helps those who help themselves," was consistently lost on the fundamentalist Big Book thumpers, whose minds were more closed off than iron prison bars. My best sponsor and friend to this day doesn't just rely on the 12-Steps, but a wide variety of daily lifestyle practices to stay clean and happy, including Buddhist principles, detachment, guided meditation, eating organic unprocessed foods, living compartmentally and systematically, and much more.

A third of the graduates from this sober living immediately relapsed within moments of leaving the facility. All were receiving the standard bullying hot seat approach as myself, to make these poor addicts *teachable*. All this method did for the overwhelming majority was to light the match toward the downward spiral, encouraging the addicts to relapse even harder. Many addicts overdosed in rehab and did not make it back, but the 12-step meetings never cared. They still do not. Their advice was to "Stick with the winners." By winners, they meant the people who drank the most 12-Step cult Kool-Aid. The recovery professionals could spout useless platitudes and repetitive slogans about how important recovery is to their lifestyle but wouldn't waste a second of energy to assist a down-and-out street alcoholic, a burned-out pothead, or a strung-out heroin junkie if they were on fire! When your message is to help the sick and suffering alcoholic or addict, yet you only help those who are already clean of their own volition and tell these poor souls that they cannot take any credit for their sobriety but can take credit for relapsing. The common slogan for this behavior is, "The program never fails, people just fail the program." Never mind the 5% statistical success rate of AA. They lie to these people and tell them they are powerless over their addictions despite their stopping or reducing drug use on their own; the recovery guru's message becomes perverted, and their questionable morality becomes punishing.

Another graduate I knew from a residential sober living began drinking again but would quit drinking independently without a 12-Step program while occasionally smoking marijuana. This individual was still holding down full-time employment, never using on the job and is doing well to this very day. He both reduced and stopped smoking marijuana on his own as well without a recovery program according to the process of natural remission where people outgrow old habits independently (Orange, 2015). This process is often weakened because of forced rehabilitation, as it lessens individual desire to change. When an addict hits bottom, it is always by his or her own admission of what constitutes a bottom for the individual. He is still, according to the 12-Stepper crowd standards, considered a failure, which is a lie and a pathetic attitude from supposed recovery promoters. If any person changes their drug habits and increases their sobriety without external pressure, it is a net positive. To condemn this person is not only close-minded, but dangerous. When the addict gets the self-fulfilling prophecy seed planted in their head that they are powerless to fight their addiction, because they are led to believe that recovery itself is a one-size-fits-all policy they will act accordingly; if they are indoctrinated enough, they will implicitly distrust their sense of self-efficacy. Yet, this is how our mental healthcare system operates and turns a serious profit. Why would you think that the people in charge of these facilities want anything altered? The people who are chronic relapsers bring the system the most money. In the words of Bill Wilson himself (Wilson, 94), "The more hopeless he feels, the better." Therefore, the system ensures the greatest number of revolving door patients are prioritized over other clients, because people who escape the regular relapse cycle do not need rehabilitation! Even at Alcoholics Anonymous meetings, with all their issues, have criticized rehabilitation centers for charging people to have access to recovery techniques offered in AA for free that do little to reduce recidivism.

The best rehabilitation center I ever went to said that recovery is never a one-way street. Several of their successful graduates were using softer drugs in a self-disciplined manner on rare occasions and staying clean at all other times. I do not promote this approach, but harm-reduction is still a better lifestyle for both the user and the people around him or her then daily living under the influence. I've tried that path multiple times and accepted that I cannot be successful at moderating my drug intake long-term before I fall apart again. For me, it is always all or nothing because whenever I controlled my drug intake in the past, I never enjoyed it in the same way as when I drank and drugged to excess. The abstinence hardliners would easily dismiss all these people who learned to moderate from past addictive behaviors as outright failures. These people who did not need dogma are happy, making lots of money, free from old addictive compulsions, and succeeding in their lives with grace, grit, and real courage. I believe that it takes true courage when dealing with any addiction to fight it from a perspective of self-empowerment because the diseased mentality that pervades America from top-to-bottom believes this is not only sinful, but scientifically impossible. That belief is purely untrue. My experience was that most rehabilitation centers in America take unnerving inspiration from fundamentalist cults and love to preach damnation for the slightest dissent. They willfully share and spread the misery to ensure that you will stay sick, needy, and dependent on these institutions to make decisions for you and take all the credit for successes while blaming the individual for all failures. The only result is a dead-end street where most people substitute addictions, without ever recovering from the addict mentality of powerlessness without personal empowerment.

As another prime example, one sober living resident who always went above and beyond to assist others in his community in order to get out of himself sponsored ten newcomers after graduating. After they all had relapsed, five of them dead from an overdose, he also relapsed. He dosed four hits of acid and then he maintained by smoking pounds of weed every day. He returned to AA and may forever continue caught in the vicious cycle of believing that AA is the only way and that he is powerless to change himself. In another situation, another recovering man had been sober for six months. He had a kind heart but was visibly struggling. During a therapy session in which he was called "an unnecessary waste of good air," the poor fellow attempted suicide in our sober living. He slit his wrists with razor blades before going on another suicidal drunk. The halfway house bathroom was covered in blood from floor to ceiling.

Sordidly, the tough love approach made me actively want to be a garbage bin for drugs, and I nearly succeeded. The only time I ever felt like I had a shred of self-worth from 2013 to 2016 was when I relapsed and pursued staying loaded 24/7; I was never clean by choice. I will completely admit I was a selfish, destructive lunatic who must have been an absolute nightmare to deal with because of being broken down by the "tough love" approach when I already hated myself and desperately needed to get built back up. All I now cared about was getting high and staying high by any means necessary, consequences damned. I awoke to yet another hellish, catatonic to the world mindset morning. My guts were twisting in the dangerous K2 spice withdrawal fires. My soul emaciated, burnt out, run-down, living at the first of many rock bottoms, dead to the entire world with a new bag of K2 Spice in my pocket, and craving nothing more than to be anesthetized into utter oblivion. I could not even bear to sit for morning meditation, so I brazenly walked out to the back of the sober living and lit up my spice pipe in the rear of the facility. Naturally, I was caught immediately after taking a few fat hits. The sober living staff responded by putting all my stuff in garbage bags and throwing me out onto the street. I begged my parents for another chance, and they were not responsive at first. This sober living had told them that I was an incorrigible pothead and hopeless drug addict who should be cut off and left to die. My parents only agreed to help me if I signed a contract saying I would never relapse again. I signed the deal, knowing that it would get me off the streets, but knowing that I did not care at that moment whether I lived or died, or had the willpower to stay clean for any length of time. I knew that another string of chronic relapses was coming soon enough. I did not care anymore about anything or anyone, let alone myself.

Arriving at the next rehab, I spent thirty days being called a jackal dope fiend of every variation and stripe. It was thirty days of straight torture until I knew the contract with my parents was void. I escaped rehab to drown my sorrows in strong alcoholic poison. I jumped over the heavily locked-down rehabilitation fence, running to a nearby 7-Eleven. My dignity no longer mattered and with desperation that rivaled Sméagol's search for his precious one ring I had the cash to anesthetize myself into a state of drunken, stoned serenity and lunacy. I bought heavily caffeinated alcohol with 12 liter ABV and expresso shots by the can and got blackout wasted on someone's private property without a second's hesitation, even puking several times violently on their garage door and their welcome mat, which must have left a grand impression. I immediately realized that I had no means to continue my run the way I wanted to and begrudgingly went back to rehab knowing I'd be busted yet again, I walked back to the rehab stinking drunk (I did not even bother to hide the stains of puke and stale beer that was all over my shirt and neck). Each time I relapsed, my treatment never changed to address any childhood traumas or depression, so the need for constant anesthesia still dominated my life.

I stayed sober for another five long and horrible months while in another sober living. This was my second to last sober living and a blessing in disguise, although sadly at this point, I believed that my future was to overdose, slit my wrists, and die alone. It mattered not. I was dead inside my soul, a black ghost of my former self. My spirit became crushed into pieces, smashed into an abyss of absolute self-loathing. I had happy dreams of shooting myself in the face with a shotgun after setting myself on fire several times a week, every week. My AA sponsor believed I was finally "teachable." I felt helpless and was willing to surrender and do whatever it took. If Alcoholics Anonymous said to jump, I asked how high. I cleaned coffee pots, arranged chairs for meetings, did my chores, sponsored newcomers, and even got a job as a retail sales associate for below minimum wage. This was not enough to stay clean, let alone happy. I completely hated my existence and every aspect of my life, and all the meetings with endless war stories kept drugs and alcohol at the forefront of my mind every millisecond. For some people, hospital & institution panels help them stay sober because it reminds them of how bad it is to be in active addiction or the degrading misery of early detox. For me, all the war stories did was to hammer the subject of drugs and alcohol onto my mind constantly. They made it impossible to build a healthy lifestyle outside of addictive coping mechanisms, feeding my perpetual revolving door cycle of relapses and regrets. The war stories always made me crave using as much or more than the desire to avoid using.

The cravings only became worse, and I did not even bother to fight the temptation to relapse. Institutional gurus said that this important battle where addicts are supposed to rely on their own use of self-discipline to control their habits or quit on their own. This thinking ran contrary to the AA dogmatic mantra of personal powerlessness, which was essential towards users' "recovery" from addiction. What a bunch of utterly malevolent prophetic garbage! To think that addicts have no volition over their right to change their behavior into whatever lifestyle they want, while telling them that they must control a behavior while admitting they cannot control themselves. This philosophy was designed for profit, personalities over principles, to weaken the wills of users, creating a steady funnel of chronic relapsers and hopeless individuals who will swallow any cruel tripe that offers them a moment of relief, but little solution or substance.

My parents sent me to numerous psychiatrists who believed the solution was to drug me up on various poisonous pharmaceuticals and SSRIs. These medications included Ativan, Gabapentin (Satan's drug of choice), and good old-fashioned reality and soul blackening SSRI's Cymbalta, and Prozac. I became so lazy on the SSRIs that I would not even swim laps in the gym for over five minutes. The SSRIs transformed me into a hollow shell of a man with a battered, emaciated soul. My higher power, sadly, was now the drugs that were supposed to keep me at baseline happiness and my growing tolerance was making that task more and more impossible. Pill after pill after pill; fix after fix after fix.

Ironically, I became a drug addict by choice to escape what I saw as a dull and superficial world, but the fast life eventually becomes **FAR** more boring than the actual world could ever be. You enter this ugly world of repetition, where all you care about is pursuing short-term pleasures at the expense of long-term personal growth and happiness. Kurt Cobain once said, "As I expected before I started doing heroin, I knew at the beginning that it would become just as boring as marijuana does. All drugs, after a few months, become as boring as breathing air" (Romance, 1). The fatalistic flaw of the addict's mentality is that pain is only evil, and pleasure is only pure, so why not push chemical pleasure buttons constantly? The trouble with this mentality is that you get withdrawal symptoms when you attempt to stop once you develop a tolerance. By now, you have conditioned yourself to need drugs to operate normally, to feel comfortable in your skin. Comfort is not bad now and then, but reliance on comfort destroys all personal growth. Only in discomfort and challenge do we strengthen as human beings and by filling those holes with drug abuse, you never learn how to deal with the stressors of life without an easy fix. When drugs are your only source of happiness, happiness becomes synthetic, and you are only miserable between hits, which is a truly disturbing and empty way to exist. You are trapped in an isolated destructive bubble, doing the same behaviors over and over associating with the same people, and performing the same activities when your life is all about getting high and staying high at all costs.

The only time you are happy in this dark universe is when you are under the influence because by then, you need your addiction to hide from the consequences of your addiction— expecting the results to be different when they never are! Yet, you feel comfortably numb and euphoric enough that you can tolerate, and sometimes even accept, a miserable existence. That is the power of drug addiction. It can rob you of your natural endorphins and happiness and to fool your brain into reliance on a state of artificial contentment! This contentment ensures stagnation nine times out of 10, even in the brightest individuals. When in the addictive cycle your body and mind are preconditioned to expect feel-good chemicals without your having to put forth any effort to get those neurochemicals naturally. This process of creating dopamine and serotonin for yourself is infinitely more rewarding and only possible to sustain through temperance and self-control. By the time the quack doctors kept adding more and more mind-altering prescriptions, I was ready to throw in the towel and jump into speeding traffic. These medications were supposed to be antidepressants. More like jet fuel for depression! None of them did anything but make my underlying clinical depression symptoms overwhelmingly unmanageable. After taking BuSpar, I became suicidal and attempted to kill myself lying in the street where moving cars raced by for thirty straight despairing minutes. My first of many more rock bottoms to follow.

When this failed, I returned to the devils calling for one last dance with K2 Spice. Since I hadn't smoked in five months, during this time the chemicals had changed from JWH to AM-694, which made the chemical vastly more hallucinogenic and dangerous. These chemicals mimic the effects of THC, but unlike THC, they can quickly kill the user via overdose. I sat near my parent's house, loaded up another bowl of insanity, and took a colossal hit! The euphoria was stronger than any drug I have ever done except for OxyCodone, and I was in heaven. I normally hated the K2 Spice high, but this was a world above any batch I had ever sampled, fifty times the buzz at a quarter of my normal pipe consumption. Instantly I was far too high, so high that every street appeared to be moving backward, as they changed color and shape with psychedelic acid tracers flying everywhere. At this point, I was walking toward my parent's house. When I arrived, I was so loaded I could not even recognize my parent's house for thirty minutes despite having previously lived there for seven years. Nothing mattered anymore. I did not give a fuck whether I lived or died. I was now the faithful disciple of the walking dead. There was zero desire for temperance, moderation, and responsible intake as this batch of K2 Spice was too strong to control. I shakily decided to stay away from K2 Spice, which resulted in one agonizing day of withdrawal; I left the dope in my drawer. When I was allowed to leave the sober living property for an appointment with another quack doctor, I knew I needed some *medicine* and finished the K2, taking two hits spaced four hours apart. I showed up at the psychiatrist smoked out on Spice. Our beleaguered session could be summarized by my telling him that if I had to take one more SSRI, I would rip the flesh from my skin with a knife and twist that knife into his chest.

By the second hit, I had majorly overdosed and was shaking and convulsing so severely that I could not hide my sordid deteriorating condition from anyone and did not care anymore. I was drug tested as soon as I returned to the sober living. So wasted I could not even speak without sounding high and out of my mind. I knew the charade was up! I had a horrible nightmare induced by the toxic synthetic flowing from my stomach to my brain. In my intensely realistic dream, I turned into a skeletal sock puppet that had maggots and cockroaches feasting on my skin everywhere I walked, an apt and ominous metaphor for the state of my now all-consuming addiction. I never used K2 Spice again. It has been over seven years, and I refuse to return to that living hell. Clearly, drugs were no longer recreational anymore. Or something for fun. They were now as necessary as oxygen and food for me to survive. My social life was nonexistent because I had abused my body and mind so frightfully with chemicals, I was a living zombie with no personality. Still, the drugs allowed me to hide from this sad, tormenting truth so well, that I convinced myself I was content, even as I was drowning under the leaden, cement-like weight of my self-destructive delusions.

CHAPTER 11

THE STREETS OR DEATH ROW

MY SPONSOR AMPLIFIED THE TOUGH LOVE APPROACH, STATING THAT my parents would drive me to skid row and leave me there to die if I did not clean up my act. I already had a dangerously severe death wish, so his method was the worst approach possible. He didn't give a fuck if he turned a profit. If this charade of lies was supposed to motivate me to change my habits, instead it prompted me to want to use drugs and die even more than ever before. For the next 90 days, I was a walking, talking husk and shut down completely. Everyone stayed far away from me because they knew I had a serious, almost pathological obsession with death. The sober living said I had to do community service or live out on the streets again. At that point, even the roads looked welcoming and inviting because I was that broken inside. I signed up for a random volunteer service but did nothing when I got there other than writing like a maniac and chain-smoking cigarette after cigarette. Writing at this moment was the only pleasure I could take out of life. The only way I felt I could keep it together, but everything else was graying out and withering away. When the sober living managers found out about my activities, I was kicked out on the streets again whilst sober—this time for good. They did not even bother to give me any of my doctor-prescribed medications, figuring that I would be dead within a matter of weeks. After four years of constant, ugly, tough love rehabs, galaxies of mind-bending prescriptions, and innumerable thoughts of suicide I could not wait to get stoned. I was tripping and wasted, deliberately out of my mind this time with nothing to stop me from destroying myself and everyone who dared stand between me and my deceptively false source of happiness and comfort. Now getting loaded was the only life I had left.

This began my descent into severe drunken, stoned, fucked-up insanity and psychosis for another long and very dark week. I went to my best friend's house and sadly conned his mother out of whatever money she could spare. I walked to a homeless shelter, beaten to within an inch of my life by cocaine hustlers' seconds after arriving on Venice Beach. I have no recollection of what these men looked like, as I was in such a blackout, broken, and empty state inside. I wished they would end my misery and finish the job they started. I was consumed with total apathy and overwhelming self-hatred. I spent nearly all the money on alcohol, pills, and Cannabis. The surrounding homeless alcoholics were loading up on tall cans of Four Loko and beer; I downed them all over the next few hours. All my belongings filled garbage bags that I kept in a rusty old shopping cart, covered in urine and hobo feces. This tragic moment was what my life, which had been filled with potential and unresolved dreams, had become. I was homeless and loaded, with no hope of living or caring to live to see another day.

I stared at the ocean in waves of morbid longing, wondering if I should go for a dip in a riptide and never return to land again. That night, it poured torrential rains that covered every street and every graffiti tagged signpost, all of which were covered in luxurious, eloquent profanities. I slept in mental and physical agony outside my parent's house underneath a damp, piss-soaked blanket. The cops approached and told me I had to vacate the premises, or I would get arrested. One street corner was as good as another to die. Broken, battered, and suicidal, I walked back to the beachfront, pushing my shopping cart filled with everything I owned. I had a plan. I would drop off all my stuff on the beach in a deserted corner, then swim in the ocean until I ran out of energy and drowned. I was entirely persuaded that my family and the entire world would be better off without me alive.

———————●———————

At this twilight hour, moments away from death, God intervened and saved me from certain destruction. I came across a group of stoners and an ex-meth user who had been clean two years from meth by using Cannabis. The marijuana maintenance program is controversial to this day but works for some as a temporary bridge towards sobriety. "Hey man, you look like you're in a tight spot." I sensed a friendly spirit within the man, which made me feel human for the first time in three years. But my self-hatred had reached its boiling point. "Oh, don't take pity on me." I cried, "I'm not worth fucking shit, I'll never be worth a shit! Please just let me die!!!" The man paused, smiled warmly, and said, "Everyone is worth something when they choose not to give up on themselves." We then smoked a bunch of marijuana laced with salvia. As I walked towards the beach, I felt a curious sensation within as my ego was annihilated; I became one with the ocean and the sandy landscape. As the salvia took over, my newfound desire was to eliminate my drinking, cease my habitual Cannabis use, and get sober; thoughts I could never have fathomed before. The salvia experience was the first time in three years I could see myself beyond my demons, beyond my bad behavior as a human being into a state of neutrality where I could objectively observe my soul and my intentions. I had to fight and eliminate the belief that I fundamentally did not deserve to be happy in life. I thought that this morbid reality directly resulted from my selfishness and self-destruction. Therefore, I had believed that I needed to do penance for excessive chemical indulgence with a shitty and dark lifestyle for eternity. And yet, I had an epiphany that this belief system was at the core of my addiction and not of myself.

Even then, I did not realize that my problem was not drugs, but a lack of self-discipline, except for my writing, and my lack of emotional maturity which stunted my life. People with mastery of those concepts will never get addicted to anything. I believe that people without self-discipline and emotional maturity will only know self-inflicted misery, isolation, and self-deception. I fully blamed myself for agreeing to move away from my hometown and letting myself go to rehab years later without suggesting alternatives. I blamed the bullies who physically assaulted me and set off my PTSD. I blamed those who were my educators, for not questioning my principles and encouraging me to pursue other fields of study as alternatives, which would have assured a higher income for me without sacrificing my creative inclinations. I should have blamed myself for using drugs and alcohol not for consciousness expansion, but to specifically deaden my senses and compromise my values. Yet, I willingly let drugs deplete these resources time and time again. I blamed everything and everyone else but myself, my pitiful and loathsome ego, and my delusional escapist mindset and self-destructive behavior that ran rampant since I was twelve years old, because it was **ALL** about me: my pain, my troubles, my trauma, my feelings, my sorrows, my happiness. By default, I care more for others than myself and I fight to change this because if I cannot love myself or take care of myself, I cannot love others, nor give to others. Yet I was consumed in selfishness and self-seeking, willing to endanger the welfare of my friends and loved ones all for another score, another hit, another fix where one is too many and a million never enough! No wonder I was alone, strung-out, and miserable. Who would want to tolerate a self-destructive twat like that? No wonder my friends stopped talking to me. In that state, I was not the kind of person who could ever handle a serious friendship, let alone an intimate relationship. Two people cannot have a consistent or interdependent relationship when one of them is a junkie, because to the addict, drugs or their behavioral addiction are the priority, nothing and no one else. You do not need to shoot heroin, smoke marijuana, or do any drugs to be an addict either. Suppose you prioritize any behavior (even virtuous behaviors) to the point where it is an addiction that forces you to compromise your values, and your balance. With your intense interests, friendships, relationships, and your conduct around other people, you are still an addict if your behavior is more important to you then yourself or the well-being of others. It is when addicts clean up their act (if they live long enough to do so), that they realize this barrier between themselves, and others must be destroyed to have a happy and fulfilling lifestyle.

For the first time in years, I also felt a moment of profound peace on that derelict beach. What appeared as a ghetto shantytown was a mental oasis from years of suffering, a harbor of sanity in a sea of self-inflicted madness. I realized I was an addict and that if I did not change my life and come to terms with my demons, my demons would inevitably destroy me. The salvia trip only amplified the intensity of this notion. Like a metaphor of the life, I had been living, my hallucinations were of the ocean transforming into a sea of Scotch whiskey, thousands of dead skeletal fish floating at the surface stripped to the bone. As each fish took a drink of whiskey, I watched their gills and skin peel down to the bare bones, burn into piles of ash, and melt away at the bottom of the ocean. I could no longer live my life in a state of denial. Although I had tried to live by ignoring the signs of my demons for several more disastrous years, it seemed almost impossible to realize how isolated, embittered, and empty I felt inside. That emptiness finally supplanted my love of the drugs and alcohol with a hatred of my escapist mentality. This hatred was strong enough for me to change my habits.

I still love drugs and alcohol despite vowing, God-willing, never to touch them ever again. Drugs and alcohol were never at fault for anything that happened to me. Drugs have no consciousness; they do not force themselves upon people. Users force drugs upon themselves. The sole individual to blame was myself, for my lack of self-control and self-discipline, feeding the mental obsession with escapism that almost destroyed my life! My mindset led to my addiction more than the drugs themselves, and I have found this true for most addicts. Most addicts, when completely sober, still describe their mindset as a dry drunk. I found this belief self-limiting. Once you treat the underlying philosophy and mental health symptoms, the habit often fixes itself. Other alcoholics and drug addicts on the street clothed me, gave me food and shelter, and treated me with more compassion, love, and kindness than at any of the rehabs I experienced. They offered more caring than any addiction professionals ever could or ever would to any of their patients. As an active or ex-junkie will tell you, even a great many doctors have a seething hatred of opiate addicts (junkies specifically) and view them as subhuman POS's, a direct violation of the Hippocratic Oath, "Do no harm."

I have become steadfastly convinced that the only reason I did not die was for three crucial reasons. My passion for writing and music and a deeply ingrained sense of belief in God never faltered, even as I lost faith in myself many times. My overall preference for psychedelics and then, as I got older my preference for complete abstinence overcame the craving for habituating narcotics. Due to my inevitable wake-up call, which involved full-blown delirium tremens from hard liquor binges, one year after my week on the streets and several more failed rehabs, I could no longer drink and use without consequences like in the old days. Another wake-up call would follow in 2017 to 2019, which would lead me to quit my Cannabis consumption and abandon my stoner image for good, an event I once never, **EVER** thought would happen in my lifetime. Marijuana was so ingrained in every facet of my daily routine as a writer and as a human being. I was so accustomed to making top-marks academically and working while stoned out of my mind, that I thought the drug could never turn on me, no matter how much weed I blazed up. Naturally, I was **PROFOUNDLY** wrong. People who tell themselves that a behavior isn't a problem, already know how badly their problem has already spiraled out of control. It's about denial, not just to save face but to avoid the discomfort of confronting the inevitable wreckage that comes from addiction.

At one point, rather than go to a rehab I was sent to a detox ward. There I was dosed up with so much Valium and Thorazine that I appeared to be clinically insane. I ripped a shower curtain to pieces and screamed at trees for hours until I was forcibly escorted off the property as a danger to their facility and sent back to living at my parents' house yet again! How defeated and demoralized I should have felt living with my family halfway to thirty years old, but I was so out of my mind on drugs by this point that apathy had become a way of life. Nothing mattering ever except for the next score, the next hit, the next fix, the next several hours of synthetic relief, chained to a towering avalanche of emptiness and regret. After several more vodka drinking binges, popping any pills I could find, and sneaking hits of marijuana here and there, I went to one of my last rehabilitation centers.

Here, a man who had been drinking for thirty straight years roomed in the same ward as me. He was suffering ghastly, seizure-inducing active delirium tremens, and he believed gangsters would murder his entire family. Did this rehab give him a proper detox or any proper medications? **FUCK NO**. He beat me repeatedly as I slept nude, clutching bloody coiled fists, thinking I was having sex with his wife. I awoke to the sight of a 300-pound man, towering muscles, with the flames of vengeance in his eyes. **"DID YOU FUCK MY WIFE IN THE ASS?! YOU FUCKED MY WIFE!!! YOU ARE A FUCKING SON OF A BITCH!!! I'LL FUCKING KILL YOU WHERE YOU STAND!!!"** I scampered out of the room like a puppy with its tail between its legs. He chased after me in a fury up the stairs, but he fell on the middle step and broke his nose. The rehab told me I could press charges and they would send the man to prison for the rest of his life. I was filled with fear and sympathy for this kind soul buried beneath an ocean of self-inflicted mental chaos. I could not even imagine turning the man in since I had heard him talking to his family on his iPad. I realized he was a warm soul with a severe affliction like me. I begged for them to give him a proper detox, and they complied. I hold no resentment against the man and hope he is alive and living well.

I spent several months recuperating in my parent's house yet another merry-go round of teetering between shaky sobriety and lunatic drug binges. I was withdrawing from the hospital's irresponsible doses of detox Valium, while at the same time I stole an entire bottle of painkillers from my mother. I had not any weed, so I did not care what it took to end the incessant emotional and physical pain. I knew so well the horrors that would soon follow, when an addict needs to drink and use, they need it more than anyone could ever need or want anything else. Consequences never mattered. I took a Valium by the pool one day and sat happily drowned in a narcotic stupor, convinced that I had found the solution to all my anxiety forever. I stupidly gobbled down handfuls of Valiums for days and was okay doing nothing but sitting on the porch. I was high on Valium, melting into the cushions, gazing at nothing but clear blue skies for weeks. Life was finally good again, if I didn't care about anything! Life delivered swift justice, as I was soon caught and forced to detox from the Valium. This meant violent seizures shaking up my spine and down my limbs and back, feeling like my heart would explode at any moment. Unfortunately, after detoxing from Valium and beginning what I thought would be a fresh start in a new apartment, my girlfriend used social media to reveal the full extent of her infidelities and lies. At the same time, I moved in with several roommates. They were all full-time drug users and drug dealers. Broken-hearted over the continuing drama with my ex-girlfriend—who I desperately wanted to forget—I returned to alcohol with a furious vengeance, and I smoked marijuana for breakfast, lunch, and dinner. Yet, I would soon be introduced to my true drug of choice above all others, a class of narcotics that made both alcohol and marijuana feel like a juvenile waste of good money or drugs.

It was at this point that I made an irrevocable step in my drug abuse phase. I began supplementing my massive liquor, prescription painkiller, and Cannabis intake with prescription codeine. I conned these out of a local doctor. As soon as I tried opiates, codeine, OxyCodone & the Holy Grail champagne of opiates, Opana (oxymorphone/hydromorphone). I knew without question that I had found my drugs of choice, the most valuable crutches of them all. Eating tablets of OxyContin 80s and Opanas when I was cut off which made me care less if I had codeine or not. I fell in love with death. The high was one hundred thousand times stronger than even the best marijuana I had ever smoked. When I combined opiates with weed, I entered a state of true artificial nirvana. This was a separate world with no violence, corruption, problems, or insanity, just the smell of roses dipped in honey; your skin feels like God is bathing it, and all the cares and worries of the universe no longer matter at all. It is pleasure and happiness incarnate and the veritable devil's temptation! Take the best sex you have ever had, then combine that with winning a billion dollars as you simultaneously discover the cure for cancer and become the United States President. You are not even 10% close to describing the opiate experience. Not even remotely close. The warm kiss of opiates from OxyContin and Codeine suddenly made me feel like a little boy. Everything felt fuzzy, happy, perfect, and warm for the first moments since I was an embryo.

There is a reason America is having a raging opiate epidemic. It's because the opiate high is unmatched by anything else in life. With all other drugs, including the most problematic drugs, the user can still maintain a pretense of having their soul intact. On opiates, you remain forever tempted to give your soul away because no drug or experience on Earth, not even Cannabis or psychedelics, comes close to the pure nirvana of the opiate high. Within twenty minutes of ingesting the Codeine (my first experience with opiates), I began nodding out and could not keep my eyes open for more than a few seconds. I felt like the most pleasant, happy, carefree man in all of existence! I realized Opiates are the devil's ultimate temptation without question! Everyone and everything was my friend, everything smelled of flowers I felt completely carefree. Staring at a wall suddenly held the meaning of life, and everything was entertaining! Of course, this was a set-up for the living hell of junk sickness. In the wise words of author and ex-junkie William Burroughs:

> Junk sickness is the reverse side of junk kick. The kick of junk is that you have to have it. Junkies run on junk time and junk metabolism. They are subject to junk climate. They are warmed and chilled by junk. The kick of junk is living under junk conditions. You cannot escape from junk sickness any more than you can escape from junk kick after a shot. (Burroughs, 97)

Smoking weed intensified the effects of the opiates a hundredfold, and I was wrapped in a sea of cotton wool for eleven inconceivable hours of total euphoria such as I had never known before in my entire life! As much as I craved opiates, I craved the combination as much as my own life, as it was the supreme high. Weed and opiates combined is literally another drug entirely when compared to each individually, I could never enjoy one without the other, because it was like comparing a Rembrandt or Da Vinci to preschool scribbles. Today, my craving for a rich full life is greater than my past desires, and the two cannot co-exist without the drugs taking over in the end. However, back when I was using the Canna-poppy (marijuana with opiates), I could talk to anyone and everyone and, for the first time, felt ten to twenty steps ahead of everyone in social situations. The opiates made all the negative weed paranoia vanish, while enabling me to keep the acute sensitivity and enhanced perceptions intact. Everything was fun to such an extreme it was also depressing beyond belief, because I knew that nothing in reality would ever compare, including marijuana, which now felt like a side dish instead of the main course. Marijuana has **NOTHING** on opiates both in the heaven and in the hell departments. Even staring at the wall was blissful, even if that is all that I did for ten hours. It was too perfect, too addictive and so utterly deadly. After I nodded out in less than four minutes on my bed, which felt like three hundred years of sleep in a single nap, I awoke to feel as if I hadn't had a lifetime of chronic insomnia. I felt like it had been the sleep given to divine angels as a reward for a lifetime of chastity, not intended for humanity. I awoke to a raging demon of my design and started doctor shopping for more opiates and prescription painkillers with absolute abandon.

I knew that I had found the best drugs on the planet from my first experiences first with codeine, then OxyCodone, and finally Opana, the latter being the holy grail of drugs which makes Heroin akin to baby formula. Suddenly, marijuana and alcohol were cool accessories to my lifestyle, but background treats lacking in any urgent need. Junk was another league, another world of addictive transcendental bliss. I just needed opiates, and I needed them right then and now! After drinking liters of Codeine every weekend, I began taking OxyContin during the week. One night, my roommate got ahold of 80 mg OxyContin and the champagne of opiates, 100 mg Opana. I popped four in my mouth, two of each pill. I spent the next twelve hours nodding out in synthetic heaven and knew that I was finished for life because it was far better than sex could ever be. We would space out our consumption of the opiates at first, hiding them even from our friends who took drugs with reckless abandon, many of whom heavily stigmatized opiate use. More for us! We sipped all the lean and nodded out on clouds of fake heaven on Earth while smoking weed by the ounce. I took massive rock star doses of opiates whenever I could get ahold of them, loving the ability to nod out or fall asleep in 5 minutes, instead of my average of two to three hours of psychotic insanity. I lost nearly one hundred pounds because food becomes secondary to opiates. I walked for ten miles every day to score more and more bags of yummy reality-killing narcotics until I was a 90-pound skeleton. I rarely ate over two meals a day, not caring to put healthy food in my body or any nourishment for that matter. The opiates made me so constipated, I could not pass any consistent bowel movements. I was nodding out too hard to care. I never used needles or snorted, only taking OxyContin and Opana orally and drinking Codeine in excess. Codeine was an incredible high, but relatively average when compared to OxyContin, and especially Opana.

Multitasking between my real-world responsibilities and my addiction was effortless when it came to opiates, whereas other addictions impaired me enough that the drama got in the way. What attracted me more and more to this darkness was the perfect blend of functionality and euphoria, the ability to seemingly switch between a state of sobriety and intoxication at will. This state of enhanced sobriety yet the ability to still get loaded is what makes both opiates and stimulants so addictive when compared to other drugs. I was quickly able to finish online assignments while gaming and smoking joints like cigarettes every five minutes. I did not care what anyone thought of me anymore. This was who I wanted to be for the rest of my life, smoking weed and dosing any opiate-based derivative I could get my hands on. At the time, I truly believed it, for without drugs my mind could not function with the level of overwhelming depression and apathy I experienced, which only deepened my addiction!

Sometimes I would eat only one meal a day, then drink myself into oblivion when I could not get opiates or weed, as life had become intolerable when un-medicated. Had I snorted or shot up my poppies, I would not have been alive to write this, as my daily doses ranged from 50mg to 100mg. The quantity that killed Cobain when he shot up Heroin was only 2.5mg. Heroin in the nineties was heavily cut, so users could not take large doses without risk of overdose. The only reason I could take such massive doses was that my roommates were dealers who tested the product themselves, so we had a dope fiend's wet dream at our fingertips, free and pure from the dark net without adulterants and for us alone. They would never have shared such massive doses with me had they not been raking in cash enough to give away pure dope for free! It was as natural as breathing for me as an active addict by this time. I stole those doses from them with no pity or remorse whenever they forgot to give fronts. I was not only dead broke, but in debt to several drug dealers, several of whom physically assaulted me. I never pressed charges because I needed their product and wanted to die without it; I believed that if I ended up dead, so much the better for my family. My consciousness narrowed to my solely scoring drugs before anything and everything else. My focus was to smoke enough marijuana and take enough OxyContin, codeine and Opana so that I could be sufficiently happy to even consider holding a keyboard and mouse straight. Permanent final slavery was near at hand, as no single drug could satisfy my cravings anymore, and I had to have combinations of drugs to function, let alone get high.

CHAPTER 12

SELLING MY SOUL FOR MATERIAL WISHES

THE END WAS NEAR. ALL LIGHTS WERE EXTINGUISHED. ALL ROADS pointed to my inevitable self-destruction. I discovered that a prescription GABA analogue called gabapentin made me feel, made me feel just the way smoking Cannabis would, in pill form. I became physically and psychologically hooked within days. My Gabapentin habit dwarfed even my voluminous opiate use because the pills made me want to talk to everyone for hours and I was hooked! I took 2000mg to 3000mg of the tablets every day until I realized I hated the drugs manic effect on my personality and my focus was shattered. I had to slow taper for months off the Gabapentin, because if I dared attempt a cold turkey kick, my body would feel as if I were being ripped apart as bloodied swords slicing into my stomach and intestines. It was even more addictive than opiates for me. No joke! I could not get a job because Gabapentin made everything look like a fucking cartoon. Nothing was real or mattered at all, and I did not care whether I lived, or I died anymore. If a job had a drug test, I did not even bother to stay for the interview. I even went to a second job interview fully loaded up on weed, opiates, Gabapentin, and alcohol. I knew the manager was giving me the runaround from the first interview. He was simply wasting my time out of pity, given how pathetically pale and strung-out I looked. Death would be a welcome event at this moment in my life, and I thought, a release from my forever unfulfilling existence. My potential to be snuffed out due to self-inflicted destruction that was years in the making, which tore my family apart and destroyed any ability I had to love or believe in myself as a worthy human being. I did not know what sobriety felt like anymore because I stayed loaded 24/7, buried underneath an all-consuming black sea of denial that I was happy with the way my life was going.

Factually, beneath the euphoric marijuana stupor and nodding opiate haze, I was utterly miserable and gobbling down drugs like a pig. I was deliberately hiding from the creeping realization of how far I had fallen from grace and the potentially irreversible damage I knew I had done to myself. Constantly staving off the brutal come down with more drugs, but never escaping it completely. Because I had smoked too much weed, the brain fog now followed and impaired me everywhere I went, even when NOT smoking for days or weeks at a time. The legal Cannabis industry does not tell its customers that too much consumption leads to brain fog. Unwanted side effects will linger for months and sometimes years in chronic users before they are fully sober! I now lived solely for marijuana, alcohol, and above all, codeine, Opana and OxyContin. Nothing else. I did not give a shit about my responsibilities, because I sadly believed I could not change or face reality without altering it.

So, I stayed loaded 24/7 to avoid facing this dark, morbid existence. The drugs had long stopped working as they once did because of my absolute greed and lack of self-control. My tolerance was so insane that I would have to spend a disgusting fortune to escape reality. I spent cash recklessly and without remorse, even when I could not pay rent or other expenses because I needed to get loaded to feel okay inside my skin. I needed to get loaded, essentially to escape the consequences that appeared in my life because I got loaded too often. Fundamentally, I needed my addiction to hide from the consequences created by my addiction! I was a hollowed-out mess of a human being, a profoundly black shell of my former self. Even sadder, I did not even realize what was happening to me because the drugs I was coping with were so potent they numbed me out to everything else in life!

Drugs are honestly too good to be true. Even with a high tolerance, and having to use ten to twenty times more of the drug to get the same effects because you are content, even happy with doing nothing and going nowhere at all in life. You're getting the same dopamine rush that you would from achieving your goals with none of the effort. This fact is the greatest danger of using marijuana; other drugs destroy what you are when you abuse them. Abusing marijuana, unless curbed, will eventually destroy what you **COULD** become, because you no longer utilize boredom and discomfort as motivational blueprints. Instead, the addict runs away from these sensations of growth by numbing themselves to them, stunting any hope of happiness or personal evolution. Self-control is the only way **ANYONE** who does drugs can grow; otherwise, complacency and stagnation are the only friends left. Anything else is the straight-up bullshit addict mentality of denial, which enables the user to keep using knowing that their problems are the direct result of their addictive behavior, which had become a self-fulfilling prophecy. I know because I was entirely guilty of engaging in the same rationalizations myself. Despite my intelligence, I was still a practicing addict in my twenties.

My intelligence became a crippling handicap that enabled me to excuse otherwise inexcusable actions due to my growing lack of humility and ever-increasing sense of entitlement. I watched my life completely dismantle because of these excuses and rationalizations.

The only time drugs enhanced my lifestyle was my first two years of using when I was 19 to 21 years old because that was the only time, I had any common sense and used only on weekends and was sober every weekday no matter what. That balance was perfect because I could still focus on my life goals, and the drugs did not interfere with my productivity; I used drugs as a recreational reward for clean and disciplined efforts in life. But, after those two years, I quickly made the fatal mistake of believing (because of a GPA of 3.87 and making the Dean's list) that drugs only made everything better. So why not be high on drugs and alcohol all the time without coming down? My environment in college only encouraged this rationalization. Then the dice rolled for the next eight years of my life until I quit using drugs. I say this as someone who loved drugs so much at one point that I was willing to sacrifice anything in order to continue using. Yet, I will, God-willing, not touch them ever again because the first option (temperance/discipline/moderation) is a near impossibility due to my love of the effects of being high. I desperately tried for years to achieve that the balance I had the first two years with zero success. Because I could not admit that I had crossed the line from a user to an addict, I could not uncross it. I was not using drugs during the final eight years because I wanted to, but because I needed to use drugs or go mad.

Until I stopped lying to myself about losing control over my drug use, forced abstinence for the wrong reasons was pure torture. Trying to achieve that balance (which for an addict is next to **IMPOSSIBLE**) crowded out everything and everyone else I had cared about and had loved in my life, leading to pathological isolationism. I also denied the fact that I could not have both a healthy relationship with my family and friends and continue to abuse substances. It never worked, not even once. Suppose I could have smoked weed or done drugs occasionally like self-actualized individuals (people who rarely become addicted to anything they do because of a highly developed sense of purpose and self-worth), without mind-altering substances taking over my whole life, which alienated me from my friends and family, not to mention eventually inhibiting all my life goals. If I had been a person who could have prevented my crossing that invisible line, I will fully admit that I would have continued drinking and using to this very day and would have done so happily. There was no real happiness to my experimentation with drugs, because my beginning to use was about masking and numbing a life, I already found both intolerable and terrifying. I will admit that I love alcohol and drugs, and that is why I am clean today. I realized that I love them too much, and I cannot imagine stopping once I awaken the 800-pound gorilla. Even vigilantly sober, that gorilla will only hibernate, never indeed die. Dare I wake him? He will always be hungrier than our last dance with self-destruction.

Just like most addictive personalities, I cannot moderate/discipline my drug use for a long time before I inevitably return to excessive and dangerous consumption levels. I tumble down the rabbit hole and my life falls apart once again. Sadly, I like the drugs far too much even with my life-destroying high tolerance not to become strung-out again, no matter how long I stay sober. I desire to be an authentic spirit, one who does not need drugs or alcohol to calm or influence him, because I now know that authenticity is where the most rewarding life exists. Finally, making peace with the fact I am one of that 9-10% of people who cannot self-discipline my drug intake under almost any circumstances. This was the critical attitude change that enabled me to get clean and change my life.

Mindset is everything. It determines your productivity, social skills, and your finances because it drives action or inaction. It was when I dropped my intense self-criticism and my constantly unattractive fatalistic streak that my life started getting better. My last and worst rock bottom was when I would work while using drugs on the job, often using them on the clock. I never got caught once, for I had perfected my existence as a functional addict to an exact, meticulously calculated science. I went to a new job as a retail sales associate while high on opiates and weed. I had insufflated 80 mg OxyContin and one 100mg Opana to be exact, having never gone to work high before. Snorting was a brief flirtation with opiates, but the rush was even faster than eating pills. I remember having a sales goal to meet for the holiday season. We were told to make customers like us enough to purchase in bulk, and that a promotion would reward the top performers. Sober I felt incapable of meeting this goal; sociability was beyond me by now, and I was only irritable, restless, and discontent when not on drugs. So, I went to work high on Opana, OxyContin and Cannabis soaked in 98% THC-infused wax. This combination of opiates and marijuana was the supreme high to end all highs for me, and I affectionately referred to it as my *Canna-poppy*, my greatest weakness to this day! Sure enough, I sold more product than I had ever sold in my life, talking up a fucking storm because of opiate and pot induced sociability. I desire above all else in recovery to be the champion I truly was on the sales floor that day without needing opiates and marijuana to get there.

The usual Cannabis-induced paranoia was replaced by an oceanic tidal wave of absolute calm and artificial serenity of indescribable, maliciously evil perfection. Everyone and everybody stayed my friend. I felt like a demigod; no one could say no to me, and I sold without exaggeration over a thousand dollars' worth of product. I felt like Superman and The Incredible Hulk combined! However, nodding out on the toilet during my lunch break, the self-loathing that I felt that day became profoundly unbearable. I thought of my loving father, who worked hard each day of his life to provide for us. Now his youngest son was making lots of dough but existed as a black hole garbage bin for narcotics. I felt that I would never know happiness again without opiates and marijuana combined. One or the other could not satiate the addict within me anymore. I had to have the *Canna-poppy* at all costs! Even if I could find stability and peace another way, I thought it could never compare to this artificial yet intense nirvana. I stood upon the edge of a cliff looking into the abyss, begging the devil to give me justification for an eternal plunge into a world devoid of emotions or pain; I wanted infinite nothingness, endless emptiness, and apathetic ascension to the high heavens. Willingly, I would have tainted my father's legacy forever in violent, selfish blazes of total abandon had I continued any longer in the poppy fields.

Nothing so blissful has **any** right to exist in a world as cruel as this. This world is so cruel that often fake happiness feels like the only obtainable contentment in the short term. It is equally cruel that often the most powerful euphoria in existence comes from artificial chemicals. The *Canna-poppy* combination, *Gascid* (LSD combined with Nitrous Oxide), as well as the infamous *Speedball* (heroin and cocaine combined) separates the weak from the strong by giving you the one chance to relinquish your humanity and destroy your soul in exchange for total invincibility from the human condition. These three combinations of drugs (opiates and weed, LSD and Nitrous Oxide, and/or opiates and cocaine) offer the penultimate panacea to loneliness, boredom, fear, anxiety, doubt, worry, or any problems. Once you experience these combinations, your whole existence centers around using as you are no longer shy of combining soft drugs with hard drugs. Life telescopes down to one big problem when the drugs run out, or no problem at all if enough dope is at hand. The speedball is the deadliest combination of drugs imaginable, as attempting to experience the perfect balance of stimulants and opiates has killed thousands of addicts. The *Canna-poppy*, while much less dangerous physically, is no less hazardous to the soul as it gives you the most powerful illusion of perfection. *Gascid* is just as dangerous psychologically, as many have said it's an experience better than love itself. Despite these dangers, this is the intensity of drug-induced euphoria that addicts are willing to gamble their lives on—no matter the cost, as the high is literally that incredible. It's not those drugs stop working with a high tolerance, it's that the same high you got in the beginning now costs an unfathomable fortune to get the same effect. Eventually, my propensity for narcotics caused the thousands I had saved up to dwindle, which I only regained once I became clean and sober.

Opiates and marijuana had become my master and I had become their very willing slave. I stopped using opiates cold turkey soon after my inglorious sales floor performance, using no methadone or Suboxone to taper off. My fear of opiates was greater than any other drug I had ever taken, because they did for me what no other drug could possibly do and exceeded expectations to a level where I knew that my humanity was slipping. Prior to this I did not take opiates daily—until the last two months of my habit, because by then I began experiencing junk sickness when I went without a nod. Subconsciously, I would stop using opiates for weeks to keep my tolerance low and keep the high as intense as possible. Even so, I could not bear the disturbing thought that I was finally turning into a full-fledged junkie, a suicidal lunatic who would destroy my family, dreams, and myself. I kicked my opiate addiction, a 50 to 100mg per day Codeine, Oxycodone and Opana habit cold turkey. Somehow, I never used needles despite watching the chilling and notorious *Pulp Fiction* scenes involving Heroin. I remain free of opiates and painkillers to this very day.

It's been over five years now, and that is the way it will always stay, God willing, as opiates were my greatest weakness and my greatest temptation. I would not wish the junk sickness I endured on my very worst enemy! I had no ability to get comfortable in any position without breaking out in sudden, excruciating anguish. I endured interminable hot sweats, followed by frigid cold chills, which alternated every five seconds for a solid two weeks. My excrement was covered in gushing blood because the opiates made me so constipated that I bled from my rectum for over seven months. To my surprise, this was the very moment when my life began improving, despite my belief that my existence was over and I would never know happiness again.

The aftermath of opiate dependency by now had handed me my ass, broken and suicidal, on a silver platter. I smoked pounds of weed, which got me through the initial agonizing stages of PAWS (Post-Acute Withdrawal Syndrome). Post-Acute Withdrawal Symptoms occur in recovery, despite overcoming a physical dependency that are more intense for certain drugs than others. As well, hard liquor abuse had me pinned to the floor, licking the fires of hell. I attempted to drink socially when I experienced positive moments. Unfortunately, all too often I tried drinking when I was suicidal, which was practically every single day of my tortured existence. By 2018, I could not drink without going on a binge; I was not content with a small buzz, only the strongest intoxication was sufficient, no matter the consequences. Nothing stopped my binge vodka and tequila drinking until, not one, but two episodes of delirium tremens. Ironically, the first round was worse than the second. Despite being opiate-free (and having never returned), my pot and alcohol abuse were out of control. Without opiates, I was unable to get the same euphoria I craved and had once gotten from marijuana and alcohol alone. My abuse was beyond comprehension, but after opiates the joy was never the same. Now I needed to combine my original drugs of choice with harder drugs to feel okay inside my own skin, and the lies I told myself daily about my habits were insurmountable. I was still in denial. I wanted to have my cake and eat it too. Even with a high tolerance I liked drugs and alcohol far too much, but I truly hated and despised the person that I had become. Ironically, I was enmeshed in hopeless substance abuse with a primal need for drugs that was both beyond control and all consuming—even by the seedy standards of a drug addict. I was so addicted at this point that the consequences of my drinking and using were no longer considered, nor going to remove my drive for drinking and using.

At this point, I was selfish, hedonistic, self-destructive, and easily able to ignore all my responsibilities and goals in favor of getting loaded. Synthetic happiness now took priority without my realizing it, over genuine happiness. I, God-willing, **NEVER** want to be that shell of myself ever again. I completely understand why my friends stopped contacting me over the last two years of using. I did not like myself or want to be friends with someone like me in those years, because I was only concerned with filling my mind and body with constant poison. I was irresponsible, negligent, and reckless about everything and everyone else in my life. I was so under the influence that I could not even second guess my choices. I was in a whirlpool of self-loathing, disgust, and apathy beyond sordid to behold. I had become comfortable, even accepting, of performing at 25% of my actual capacity.

That is the genuinely frightening power of drug addiction. I saw that some drug addicts, functional or at rock bottom, accepted a shitty, destructive lifestyle if they can stay loaded without hassle. Why would anyone tolerate someone who routinely preferred living in a synthetic world over the real one in the long-term? Non-addicted people may use drugs temperately, while keeping their heads on straight; they practice self-discipline without thought. My creative goals eventually became secondary to my sordid but necessary gray reality of drug misuse in order to hide from my traumas and pain. My dreams all changed to meet my delusional and lethal consumption of drugs. My energy was so fatalistic and pessimistic that I could feel the entire world moving away from me as I sought oblivion to escape this creeping horror, which I had made for myself. But ignorance in the last two years of using allowed me to escape nothing at all. I could no longer run from myself when the consequences of my behavior were staring me directly in the face! Since the age of twenty-one, my head was on another planet, eventually robbing me of the self-discipline necessary to cultivate my ambitious creative goals. I am proud to say that this fast life is no longer my life by choice!

After the physical withdrawal ceased, the ensuing depression was unbearable. I felt that without opiates, life was simply not worth living. Ironically, this belief increased my determination to quell the demons inside me, since no traditional treatments had ever done anything other than feed the raging monster in my soul. Without knowing or comprehending it, I developed a systematic approach to living my life, which eliminated the failed goal-oriented mentality. I found that living incrementally and breaking down life into bite size choices is more important than focusing on the bigger picture, because all great human accomplishments only occur when the little details take center stage. We focus so intensely on the big dreams and ideas that we fail to both appreciate and implement the small elements around us that make societal and cultural transformation possible. Taking charge in this way enabled me to craft incremental changes that have resulted in a permanent transformation and brought untold blessings into my life.

CHAPTER 13

ROCK BOTTOM

MY WRITING, ART, AND MUSIC ARE MY WHOLE LIFE. WHEN DAILY DRUG abuse began to seriously impair these passions, I knew drugs were holding me back; instead of aiding me creatively as they had in the beginning two years, which were the only ones in the past 10 years when I was not an addict. It was in early 2020 that I finally quit using after a profoundly long and very arduous struggle to convince myself to give up my old self-destructive addict mentality forever. I wish I could blame marijuana or any other drugs for my being frozen in time mindset over the last three years of my use, but I alone am at fault. Even if I didn't smoke any marijuana during those previous three years, I would have supplemented it with alcohol or any other drug or escapist behavior I could dose up as fast as possible! I was never a picky drug addict. Whatever got me insensibly loaded immediately was always my preference. My drug use would eventually end for good on my sobriety date, which is May 13, 2020.

Once you cross that line between use and abuse, your body and brain forever adjust to match. I have learned through bitter experience that these seldom uncross. I could never successfully moderate my consumption after my first two years of using drugs but denied this was true religiously because that would have meant giving up the drugs. Instead, until I was 29, I would have gone without oxygen, sex, or food. If I could use drugs occasionally and temperately, believe me, I would have done so years ago—in a heartbeat. I have found love, peace, and acceptance in admitting to myself that I absolutely cannot use without the drugs screwing over my life, through trial and bitter experiences. Once you cross the line into addiction, you do not have a choice anymore. You have lost self-control and sacrificed the potential for self-actualization or balance. It is all or nothing, and only nothing will set you free. I quit because I was too fascinated with drugs' effects to master self-regulation. It eventually took over all aspects of my life. I could finally see the severe damage only when I stopped intentionally.

Cannabis is thought to be less dangerous than alcohol and most drugs. But Cannabis is still dangerous. The only way Cannabis will stay legalized is for the stoner culture to die its well-deserved death. Marijuana's greatest danger is not the use of marijuana itself. Those who smoke pot are part of the only drug sub-culture that treats excessive and daily use of pot as entirely innocuous, harmless, even beneficial. In my opinion, we need to treat marijuana like any other drug, with both benefits and dangers. If you buy into the pothead culture, you better prepare yourself for a world of misery and hopelessly wasted potential. Pot is a double-edged sword because of its short-term harmlessness and that inherently, those who use weed cannot overdose. This non-physical lethality makes it far easier to deny the problem or deny a user's rate of consumption. Cannabis is far from harmless when misused. While I hate to admit it, weed is the #1 drug that when abused destroys motivation.

The first two years of my pot smoking career involved weekend evening toking. I ensured sobriety at all other times. When I did so, I noticed that my motivation was normal. I even excelled in all aspects of my lifestyle and goals at this rate of consumption. However, the second I fell for ganja so deeply that I stopped this conscious regulation and began smoking more than two nights a week, I had finally graduated to the motivation chainsaw of wake-and bake. It was all over for the next eight years because getting high became the motivation for activities, not an augment for the activities themselves. Weed harmed me more than all other drugs because it alone was the drug that convinced me to switch from goals being more valuable than my behaviors, to behaviors becoming more valuable than my goals without my conscious awareness of this paradigm shift. I eventually realized that daily weed abuse was severely holding me back from fulfilling my ambitions and dreams. In fact, during the last two months of my marijuana habit, my entire life fell apart all around me. Worse still, I knew that it was mostly my fault, not because of smoking marijuana itself.

I had bought into the stoner ethos which preaches that daily smoking of marijuana is innocuous; this was the driving belief behind my years of abuse. I was getting evicted, a thief had stolen nearly all my money from my bank account, and worse still, I was too faded to take notice. It was the first time in my life that my attraction to drugs became secondary to my desire for redemption and repentance, and my desire to reconnect with God. I could finally see through the haze and realized that my hardcore abuses of the drugs were eventual and inevitable detriments to the values and hobbies I believed the drugs had augmented and enhanced. Drugs and alcohol alienated me from my family and my friends, while slowly sucking all my creativity and motivation for life down the drain. Rock bottom is a cold and ruthless depression for anyone in active addiction. When you realize your ambitions and dreams change to suit your habits, its already too late. You are a prisoner now. By then, you cannot expect pity or sympathy from anyone when you've dug your own grave, as I had!

In the last two years of my drug addiction, my lifestyle can only be categorized as utterly dull, isolated, and dark. Whatever benefits I believed psychoactive drugs once held in my life had long since eroded because of my self-delusional and frightful abuse of these chemicals, especially marijuana. The ironic trick of drug use is that in the beginning, they feel beneficial and fun as hell when you are temperate, responsible, and keep your goals and priorities in line. For people who know their limits, drug use can be an augment to a rich and full life. These people understand that pleasure is not the be all and end all of life itself and that pain isn't permanent, but necessary for self-evolution. By the time you cross that invisible line from use to abuse, you've created an unstoppable pattern of conditioning and reinforcement that erases those early days when there was no price to pay. Early drug experiences are seldom repeatable without severe consequences of withdrawal. But I was past being an addict at this point. Instead, I had sadly embraced off the rails spiritual suicide.

Here is my life summary for the final two years of my addiction and why I am proud to stay clean and temperate today! Wake up, pop pills, down shots of scotch shaken not stirred, and smoke weed before even taking a shower or eating any food. Guzzle down liquor like the brilliant but alcoholic author F. Scott Fitzgerald (So) on shore leave, to cure the self-flagellating shakes and violent bouts of nausea I had to endure as the price for chemical self-indulgence. If I worked or had the day off, I smoked weed, got drunk, and popped narcotics before I did anything and everything. I found myself listening to *It's You I Adore* by Snoop Dogg and *Ganja in My Brain* by Ras Matthew thousands of times in a row every day. The same marijuana and smack druggy haze inspired my playing similar tracks while getting even higher. Stoned and alone on my secondhand desk chair, knowing I had not grown out of my false comfort zone because I did the same insanity inspired things and expected the same results while wishing things were different, solely so I could have more resources to feed my addiction! I popped painkillers like breath mints to stay awake in order to combat my constant euphoric but debilitating ganja fog that impaired me everywhere I went. I initially fell in love with Cannabis (and most drugs except for alcohol) because they initially and dramatically enhanced my creativity. By the end when my tolerance was high enough, I was not creating jack fucking shit because I was too loaded to create. In retrospect, the only reason Cannabis/drugs first improved my creative habits was because the first year was the only time, I was ever intelligent about drugs. I stayed sober every week, then used drugs on weekend nights only. If only it had stayed that way, but I loved drugs and their effects so much that they became my entire way of life without my even realizing the change in my mindset about how to achieve happiness. Then the downward spiral began! My mindset had become so dark and twisted that life without chemicals felt impossible to imagine. In the words of

Fitzgerald himself, "My vision of the world at its brightest is such that life without the use of its amenities is impossible" (So, para. 2). Marijuana makes you incredibly happy even if you are bored. However, you'll also be too comfortable to develop or grow into the best version of yourself. I believe that goes for any behavior or addiction, frankly. Balance, self-discipline, variety, healthy diet (with some comfort food sprinkled in now and then), and sufficient time and money management skills are core happiness tools.

Once I became a pothead/addict in denial, I smoked marijuana daily. I increased my intake of other drugs to daily/semi-daily abuse. Everything in my life snowballed out of control and best/worst of all, I was far too loaded to notice it until it was far too late! One hallmark of a non-addicted person is that those who engage in pleasurable activities have the self-control to remain temperate. Non-addicted people change their behavior to meet their systems, whether they use drugs recreationally or abstain entirely. Addicts have the unfortunate willingness to change their systems to match their behavior, no matter what or who is lost in the process. Systems are the 21st century version of goals, since they are a more refined process that emphasizes incremental and compartmental decisions as far more important than the big picture accomplishments, which can only generate through small choices. Addicts always fantasize about learning to control what became utterly uncontrollable for them.

I was no exception. I was in a constant brain fog day in and day out, gorging on takeout like a pig and washing it down with marijuana, painkillers, occasional hallucinogens, benzos, and liquor day after day in my isolated apartment, alone after work. I did not care about my responsibilities anymore. My neutered creativity became a means to a dead end. My goals changed during the last two years of my addiction to support my staying numb and seeking oblivion by any means necessary to avoid having to face myself and my insanely dark lifestyle. I'd gorge on more shitty takeout and roll blunt after blunting while chasing it down with more liquor, opiates, gel tabs, and pills. My friends and family wondered why I was unhappy and constantly depressed. I was not writing, nor was I drawing, creating art or music, pursuing any meaningful financial goals, being social with my friends, pursuing relationships, or any of the things that make life rich and fulfilling. Getting loaded was more important to me than anything else, because that was the only moment, I felt happy and comfortable inside my own skin. Alone in my room taking hits from the bong like Cheech & Chong, listening to the same music religiously that encouraged my sordid habits. It was pure hell, disguised as heaven, and the hilariously disgusting part is that the drugs were still giving me an intense experience euphoria. Given my access to narcotics, there was no cap on my tolerance as I always got the high, I wanted, no matter what it took. Drugs were fooling me into thinking I was enjoying myself and content with my lifestyle when, I was borderline suicidal knowing I could not face reality without augmentation.

At this point, I became addicted to my addiction, addicted to using the drugs to self-medicate the pain caused directly by drug misuse. Once you hit this cycle, moderation or temperance becomes impossible and it's abstinence or death. You have epigenetically reprogrammed your consciousness into a dysregulated process of conditioning and reinforcement. The same behaviors that brought ease and comfort at first become ineffectual without a massive increase in the dose (AKA tolerance). Due to increased intake, your withdrawals also increase unless the behavior is significantly reduced or better yet outright eliminated! Clearly, this is not exclusive to drugs but is true when considering all behaviors that release dopamine and serotonin. Sugar is an excellent example, as a dopamine agonist that spikes dopamine rates with habitual intake (Avena et al.). Too much dopamine leads to addiction, while too little serotonin leads to depression in most cases.

I was content with performing and existing at easily 25% of my true self, living without living. I would not go back to that miserable existence if you paid me big money to abuse drugs again because it was sadder and darker than anything else in the world and I refuse to return! I cannot use drugs in moderation/temperance as many other people can, and I could not care less about my inability to do so. I will always be an all or nothing person. Clean & sober, my life now has potential and joy again, and I refuse to snuff it out for anything! My spirit had become dampened into an abyss of addictive repetition. Smoke good, eat good, drink good, think I am living right, but far too fucked up to realize how miserable my existence had become, how not right in every category. So, what's the moral of this story? In the wise words of Kurt Cobain, who perfectly described this dark cycle, "All drugs after a few months, become as boring as breathing air, but you still need to do them" (Romance, 1). Also, for anyone who says marijuana is only psychologically habit-forming, I can confirm that when I finally quit, I had mild physical withdrawal symptoms that were quite irritating, although a cakewalk compared to alcohol, tobacco, and especially opiates.

From 2018 until early 2020, I lost all motivation to do anything even semi-productive unless stoned out of my mind. Once my tolerance was high enough, my motivation only reached a baseline of inspiration. When sober my motivation existed as an ugly flat line, which I preferred to self-medicate with drugs, rather than deal with the problem. I was craving a drug to prevent the craving of other drugs. I was craving my addictions to hide from the problems directly caused by my addictions. My creativity, once aided by drugs, was nonexistent underneath the foggy, self-deceptive haze. I could not hide from the fact that the medicines which once increased my creativity and my motivation for success had turned me into a listless, apathetic burnout with none of my characteristic drive that had allowed me to graduate in the top 1% of my university. I had become everything I swore I would never allow myself to become and hated my entire existence!

Numbing the pain never works because you never learn how to deal with and accept that pain as a part of life and a part of success. You cannot feel high without feeling low. Your problems are still there, no matter how high you get the next day! There is no hiding in my life, not anymore, or ever again. I even began getting withdrawal symptoms when I would try to stop only assuaged by the combination of Valerian Root and Saint John's Wort—a must-have for all Cannabis abusers looking to regain control of their lives! I knew I had to either permanently level out my Cannabis use or abstain completely. Drugs always took over my life eventually, regardless of my intentions. By the end of my drinking and using, I had to painfully admit to myself that I still enjoyed the drugs tremendously. Recovery gurus had completely lied about drugs not being fun again after a period in recovery. Still, I came to loathe and despise the person that I had allowed drugs to mold me into, infinitely more than I enjoyed the escape and relief that drugs had always provided me. Until that mindset changed, I could not break my addictions, especially my daily marijuana abuse, which had become far more than an addiction, but a way of life. From 2019 to early 2020, I felt like I could not function or be happy about anything without being stoned. The irony was that the drugs now increased my depression and self-hatred with every dose. I also began getting panic attacks and horrifying paranoia when stoned or sober! It was only after quitting weed for good that the paranoia has subsided, and although I will always love Cannabis, God forbid I ever go back to smoking weed every day.

I prefer being creative when I am clean and sober, so now I'm able to write and create music without needing to alter my mind. I cannot forget the lessons I learned as a writer and as an artist in college from my drug use, as they were invaluable. My childhood was the time that I formed an addictive and severely unhealthy relationship between comfort and discomfort. Everything was taken care of for me as long as my grades were excellent, so I lost the ability to both take care of myself and seek new experiences, due to an attraction to sameness—the opposite of change. It took the suffering, misery and the pain of addiction for me to slowly but fundamentally realize that comfort holds no growth or happiness without changing one's relationship to discomfort from a burden to an opportunity. I have seen that overcoming adversity leads to moments of great pleasure. For me, it became time to change and move on from my turbulent past, constructing a brighter, happier future for myself, one where drugs are no longer the sole focus of my whole life; they no longer have any place in my life. I regret nothing about the lessons that drugs taught me. Yet, to continue drinking and using would be to live out a self-destructive lie. It would mean allowing an external force to block off my potential for genuine happiness, while choosing long-term damage and deficits, which I refuse to accept as my lifestyle anymore! Being a drug addict is not living. It is always living while dead. It is living to seek the deadening of your senses and alter the world into something it is not to mitigate pain. But by avoiding pain, you also prevent joy and happiness!

Life is all about balance, both in emotions, attitudes, and behaviors! I pray I will never forget the struggle and sacrifices I made to get clean and live temperately. Unlike non-addicts, my mentality when using or engaging in any addictive behaviors (drugs not required) is to fight that balance. Avoid any pain and only feel pleasure at all costs, an attitude that has only brought untold misery into my life for nearly a decade! I would blame this mindset for seeking only pleasure, for most if not all my problems since I was twelve. Attitude determines the outcome, and since middle school, I chose isolation and had a fatalistic view of the world. I believed that I had to change the way I viewed the world to tolerate reality—chaining myself to paralyzing comfort zones that eventually inhibited my creative and spiritual growth, until I cleaned up my act for good. It is not drugging or any comfort-inducing behavior that is bad if you have the self-discipline for self-restraint and equilibrium. Still, when you make it a lifestyle and a coping mechanism to deal with the reality that the addiction kicks off, you enter a living hell. The addict will inevitably lose everything unless they change course.

Although my addictive lifestyle was primarily my fault, I also feel like my education sadly lacked an explanation for why self-restraint and discipline are essential to success. Telling our children not to do drugs does not solve the demon of addiction because anything can become a destructive addiction. Tolerance and withdrawal symptoms are not exclusive to drug addicts. Just ask anyone addicted to sugar. It is the new crack cocaine! We cannot have future quality education for future generations that do not include a focus on harm reduction or classes on why self-restraint and discipline are more valuable than intelligence for sustained success in the adult world. We are cheating the next generation out of any sustainable future. I was taught general education topics in school, but the curriculum didn't include any of the habits or the mindset needed to cultivate long-term success in the cruel and unpredictable modern world. Those I had to teach myself! And I had to learn it through the worst way possible which I would not wish on anyone—full-blown drug addiction and alcoholism.

I cannot forget that night of horrid delirium tremens that nearly obliterated me near the end of my sordid drinking career. At that point, I would drink several beer cans and vodka bottles like they were water. Morning drinking had become routine in 2018, and I refused to eat anything until I got drunk. As I was staring at the ceiling of speckled marble shifting ablaze with red flashes, a volcano erupted in my direct vision from the hanging lampshade. I was consumed in my walled marble prison of self-effacing shame and loneliness. The bathroom mirror turned into a demonic creature, spewing out pedophile rapist ghosts who screamed endlessly, "Time to rape you with toast and jam, time to rape you up petty bitch!" for eight straight hours. Millions of ninja lizard throat cutters slowly crept up to my windows, smiling while offering pies filled with bottomless holes of atom bombs. Even tripping on Salvia did not make me lose sight of reality to such an astonishing degree. On marijuana or psychedelics, even experiencing ego death moments, I still knew that it was the effects of the drug that was causing me to trip, and a Valium will bring things down if you have an unpleasant trip on acid or shrooms. However, when engulfed in delirium tremens, the message was clear. I was not on drugs anymore. This state was my insane reality. I would be psycho ward wet-brained and insane for the rest of my natural life. In a state of delirium tremens, I knew that

I would die young, ruined by alcoholism. By hook or by crook, I stayed seated on my bed, crossing my legs in a meditative stance to lessen the delirium demons inviting me to embrace the sweet kiss of death. Although I woke up alive, I still used hard alcohol for one last binge before giving it up. I followed by nearly four more years of decreasing beer consumption until I finally quit alcohol for good.

After crapping my pants during a diarrhea episode, I tossed my pants into the washing machine, accidentally destroying my wallet with my obliterated driver's license inside. I burst into my parent's bedroom filled with self-hatred and thousands of demons; they had locked their bedroom door (with adequate moral reasoning, given that all the alcohol was kept in there). I somehow picked the lock successfully and found Fitzgerald's version of heaven on Earth. A sea of whiskey, vodka, tequila, wine, and countless bottles of beer surrounded me. I drank nearly all the alcohol in the room in a three-hour alcoholic binge straight from the depths of hell itself. I downed the hard liquor first, guzzling down tequila straight from the bottle until I puked in my parent's toilet. Then I went right back to cracking open beer after beer after beer and chugging each bottle, guzzling wine and vodka until I got the hardcore spins and passed out into oblivion. I woke up and was busted immediately, yet I hated myself so much that I knew it would not make me stop drinking. Since that day, liquor never gave me the same kick again and my desire to get drunk slowly ebbed. There are still days that I think about drinking. However, I know that if I started drinking again, I'd begin smoking weed and using drugs again. My next bottom would be death. I do not know if I have another recovery in me, due to the severity of the way I like taking drugs. I cannot use alcohol to stay away from other drugs. Alcohol only makes the cravings for drugs even more intolerable!

I indulge in my passions constantly, writing 24/7, only stopping at nightfall! I limit video games and YouTube to late evening after completing all productive activities, as these behaviors fueled my tendencies to procrastinate for years, holding me back. One week when I nearly drank again, even taking a bottle off the shelf in a liquor store and looking at it longingly, I managed to refrain. I am a proud member of SMART recovery, a recovery movement comprised of open-minded individuals who embrace a harm-reduction and self-empowerment foundation of recovery.

In utter despair and desperation, I chose to participate in an offshoot of the SMART recovery group. I entered the facility still drinking every day but had smoked weed only twice per week. To my credit, in May of 2020, after an exceedingly long and arduous struggle, I gave up marijuana God-willing for good! It was never the fault of the Cannabis plant—the responsibility was all mine. My greed and lack of self-control and self-discipline led me to all my problems. It only was by facing down the old me and gently letting him go that I have strengthened into who I am today. During this time, I had already stopped drinking for 300 days. When I inevitably drank again, I didn't go back to the normal binge drinking of the past, because SMART inspired an attitude of self-empowerment. Eventually, I was able to cut back dramatically on my alcohol consumption, finally giving alcohol up for good. For the first time in my life at SMART, I could tell the story about my past feeling no shame or self-loathing. This healing environment was of exceptional value in setting the stage and helping me to feel more open about both childhood trauma treatment I desperately needed and my commitment to recovery.

Frankly, I have observed that most rehabilitation centers work by attempting to shame the addict into changing their behavior, which **ONLY** reinforces more addictive behaviors for 90% of patients. I already felt deep self-loathing and self-shame for being an addict, but that only made my addictions more powerful. Most addictionologists know well of this mentality with most addicts and use it to disempower people and keep the money flowing into their pockets by keeping us addicted, both to drugs and to rehabilitation centers. In contrast, the people running the SMART clinic made me feel like a worthy and lovable human being. They said I was brave to come forward and want to relinquish feeling powerless over my life. I wanted nothing more in my entire life than to shed the paralyzing dogma that encouraged me to turn into a subhuman shell. I desperately wanted to begin living life to the fullest again, which I finally did in 2020 when I hit rock bottom! By 2020, I had quit drugs entirely. I could only see apathy, grunge, and self-destruction in what I once loved deeply, because so much of my connection with the world was through the dark side of my constant substance abuse. I kicked opiates and prescription painkillers cold turkey and abandoned all other hard narcotics. My binge drinking and daily pot smoking continued at first, but the same kick I once got from these substances had long abated.

For the first time in my life, I felt at peace. Sobriety is a natural happiness most healthily maintained through personal self-empowerment, which is the best kind of happiness! I use a combination of herbal supplements, to proactively treat my clinical depression and hardcore insomnia. These supplements have worked wonders for me, because they eventually removed my need to smoke Cannabis as a coping mechanism! With guidance you can find the supplements that will work for your specific needs. I highly recommend supplementation, along with proper diet, guided meditation, and exercise, for any daily weed smokers looking to make a change or people who suffer from severe depression. It is a genuine challenge to avoid temptation in a world filled with promoting a lifestyle of excess, but each day it gets easier, one day at a time. Abstinence and extreme temperance from Cannabis consumption, alcohol consumption, and refraining from other drugs are three of the single most important choices I make every day currently to stay happy, whole, alive, and valuable to humanity.

The addiction demon is never far behind me. God forbid I let him back in. He won't stop until there is nothing left of my soul for him to take, while he continues to demand more. Therefore, constant vigilance and self-restraint which prevents the dangerous nostalgia about "the good ole days" when I was drinking and using are the prices I must pay for my freedom. The difference is I shed the disempowering 12-step model and took responsibility for my own choices to embrace recovery. I do so through self-empowerment, entrusting myself to get the life I deserve, and not seeing it as giving up something enjoyable. During the last year of my using and drinking, enjoyment had nothing to do with getting high anymore. I was self-medicating to hide from the consequences caused by my substance misuse by then, which is a corkscrew downward spiral. At this point, it is not jails or institutions that are left for the low-bottom addict. Only death by addiction or surrender to the choice of recovery awaits.

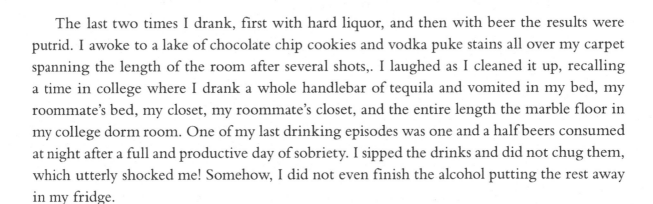

The last two times I drank, first with hard liquor, and then with beer the results were putrid. I awoke to a lake of chocolate chip cookies and vodka puke stains all over my carpet spanning the length of the room after several shots,. I laughed as I cleaned it up, recalling a time in college where I drank a whole handlebar of tequila and vomited in my bed, my roommate's bed, my closet, my roommate's closet, and the entire length the marble floor in my college dorm room. One of my last drinking episodes was one and a half beers consumed at night after a full and productive day of sobriety. I sipped the drinks and did not chug them, which utterly shocked me! Somehow, I did not even finish the alcohol putting the rest away in my fridge.

CHAPTER 14

EMOTIONAL & SOCIOCULTURAL RECOVERY

I NOW REALIZE HOW FOOLISH AND GROUNDLESS MY DESTRUCTIVE beliefs were. I know today that to love others, I must love, discipline, and care for myself as I would for others. I use an incremental systematic approach to change multiple habits, not just my drug use, including my overreliance in 2017 on eating out and binging at I-Hop on far too many pancakes. I began buying groceries when low on food to save money incrementally. The only change that can make successfully is through an incremental approach. Now I keep a journal of my intake for constant accountability of the substances I put in my body. I use an application called Habit Bull to track my consumption and stay self-disciplined so that old habits never take over my life again.

———————●———————

I exist in a complete 180° turnaround of my life, from a man who should be, and scientific inquiries remain dead—a man who should have died thousands of times over. Now I prefer to stay clean at all costs. I have never felt more alive, centered, or content in all my existence. I could not even be clean at all for five minutes over half a decade upon waking up at six in the morning, let alone all day for years and years living in the continuous fast lane. I was always near broke despite the intelligence to make a living, barely eating food, and wasting away into a shell of a man. Nor did I have any desire to practice self-control in any of my habits because the only way for years I could tolerate myself was through a haze of excessive drug consumption in my twenties, always seeking oblivion. What enabled me to kick drug abuse to the curb was realizing that I seldom enjoyed the experience whenever I controlled my drug intake. Whenever I enjoyed taking drugs, I never managed my drug intake. Non-addicts who take drugs in moderation or prefer never to suffer from this crippling duality as addicts suffer. All addicts live with a duality nature. They are two types of people who are always in perpetual conflict with each other. The war between the addict who has a conditioned mind and the person inside them is a battle between the impulses of the lower-base brain vs the cognitive reasoning of the higher brain.

Theirs is a love-hate relationship, not just with themselves, but with their addictions of choice. They love the relief; they hate the consequences. They hate the damage to their loved ones but love the ability to escape from a life that feels emptier than the fear of hurting others. They do it without thinking and can enjoy themselves without losing themselves. Because every other day, a part of me obsesses about controlling what became uncontrollable, I know I have lost that ability and that right to drink or use for good. It is for the best! I have never wanted to use drugs temperately and never will use drugs moderately long term. Even with 30 years or more clean and sober, that will never change for me. I love the effects, euphoria & escape far too much, and it turns me into a demonic imposter who is not remotely Skyler Pennington anymore, as the moment I give in, I am over and destroy everything in my path. The only time I can think of that I used drugs moderately/temperately/beneficially was my first year of operating, starting at twenty years old. That was when my life remained balanced despite my pot-smoking, drug experimentation and drinking with friends. My goals and hobbies, which initially tempered my habits to responsible and sensible levels, eventually fell by the wayside in favor of rampant drug abuse until early 2020, made the wise decision to kick drugs to the curb forever. That one year is the template by which everyone who experiments with drugs must adhere or suffer accordingly and lose everything. That one year was also the only year drugs enhanced my creative process, and sadly I believed that if they did so as a faithful weekend warrior, why not be on drugs and alcohol all the time? As soon as I crossed that line, my creativity slowly but surely numbed and degraded into 25% of my actual capacities, and my entire life fell apart as an active addict until I made that realization and decided to quit. People can scream at a drug addict how insane and destructive their behavior is for years on end. Still, until the addict truly sees it and feels the consequences of their self-destructive behavior within their heart and soul, nothing will ever change for anything. Nothing changes if nothing changes.

Drugs do not ruin your life because they are wrong. Honestly, the tragic truth is **NOTHING** in the world has **ANY** right to be as unique and powerful as drugs are. Nothing else can make you feel like a king of a small continent even when your life is in the gutter because of your own choices, make you think you are at the Ritz getting head from a thousand people at the same time even when your skin broke and cannot rub two nickels together. Drugs have the magical, almost superhuman ability to make nothing feel like nirvana, no matter how shitty your circumstances. That is why dope fiends and addicts fully accept the shitty nature of their lifestyle. The pleasure from the high is so intense that they can tolerate the most insane circumstances happily, if the dope is potent and stays flowing by any means necessary. Perhaps it is genetic because my uncle struggled with substance abuse when he was alive. I also realized that my lack of self-control made it impossible for me to focus on the people or goals I cared about because of my excesses. I wanted to have my cake and eat it too and could have, having gone into drug experimentation with an attitude of temperance, self-discipline & responsibility. But outside of writing, I always lacked self-discipline because I foolishly believed that if my work was quality, what did life basics matter? I have become humbly forced to realize that you will never know success if you do not have the basics. Who wants to take advice from someone who does not practice self-care? I soon learned I loved the euphoric escape of drugs so much that I cast my responsibilities aside eventually in favor of getting loaded, which ordinary people, even those who indulge, avoid. I am disciplined as a writer and as an artist. Still, my addiction experiences taught me I have an equal number of undisciplined habits to correct or eliminate to live a happier and healthier lifestyle.

My heroes lived in addictive excess, so I rationalized living my lifestyle in addictive luxuries and suffered the full consequences accordingly. But then I realized the high, life-threatening price their addictions dealt. My role models frank about these sacrifices. I changed my beliefs about drugs and alcohol to adapt to the changing world around me. Just as I abused substances when I felt I had no reason to live, I became clean and lived a more self-disciplined lifestyle for the same reasons. I refuse to compromise anymore on being the best and going where ordinary people refuse to go, living my life in a way other are afraid to live, under all consequences and circumstances, but sober. The difference is, now I have everything to live for, healthily and happily. I have ceased to believe in any notions of powerlessness over my body and my life! Self-actualized addictions and passions now include far more than psychoactive chemicals! My love and passion for music and writing grow every second and make existence worth living for me. My passion and love for life have returned without the numbing hand of opiates, liquor, and prescription painkillers to rob me today of my growing spirituality. I used to live in years of darkness, yet now even the darkest moments of my present existence do not awaken the chorus of demons which once ruled over my life with an iron fist of malice and determined self-destruction.

My life is far from perfect by any measure, but it is better than it has ever been before, despite the many temptations I resist every day! They are sometimes in the background, and they may never go away for as long as I live. Today, I consider them a privilege and a blessing, for they motivate me to strengthen, and they force me to learn the value of pain and discomfort as a creative writer and digital artist. There are still days that I struggle and moments where I crave going back to old patterns of everyday drinking and drugging. However, I have embraced a sober lifestyle wholeheartedly and of my own volition. I know for a fact, that I will die unless I steadfastly make this way of life a part of the very foundation of my being. I am now enjoying an existence where I always stay 100% accountable for what goes into my body and mind. Now have more self-respect and a passionate fire that will never stop burning until I transform the landscape and language of mental health and addiction forever. I have since realized that when you play with fire, without self-acceptance and a willingness to change, eventually you will get burned. Sobriety does not make people immune to close-minded, selfish, or even self-destructive decisions. I have since realized that drugs and alcohol themselves are rarely, if ever, the central source of an individual's tendencies towards addictive behaviors. The addiction is merely a surface behavior based on underlying and far more severe psychiatric issues. I've observed that in the recovery subculture, particularly within Alcoholics Anonymous, one of the most grating and self-destructive issues is the separation of the entire logical spectrum of healthy human emotions, both in the negative and positive range. Alcoholics and addicts who attend 12-Step meetings stay stuck constantly yammering about the *disease of self*, and how they need to feel serenity and gratitude all the time. They are encouraged to think that anger and resentments themselves are poisons that directly cause a relapse. Pages 88 to 95 of the Big Book texts state specifically:

> "It is a spiritual axiom that every time it disturbs us, no matter what the cause, there is something wrong with us," notes the author of *Twelve Steps for Twelve Traditions*, another core text for people in recovery. "If somebody hurts us and we are sore, we are in the wrong as well (Alcoholics Anonymous, 88-95)."

Given this demented logic, a woman who gets brutally raped must own her wrongdoing. Children who watch their parents murdered through no fault of their own are spiritually sick for being disturbed by those events. Even if someone cuts in front of you while you're standing on a line to get into a club, and you experience a moment of annoyance—you have failed to demonstrate AA's required humility (dangerous self-effacement)! In recovery myself, I have found that accepting and loving all of my emotional states is crucial to my long-term health, maturity, and happiness. Looking back, my first (and least effective) AA sponsor taught me that at my core I had to both hate and fear my emotions and attempt to replicate a neutral serenity state without intense emotions. I came to believe that any feeling other than constant serenity and gratitude would lead me to relapse. This would lead me back to abusing drugs and alcohol time after time, when the 12-Steps alone failed to produce this state despite working the steps three different times consistently.

Without effective childhood trauma therapy and the processing of my past, in direct correlation to embracing detachment from both my past desires and self-image, recovery was merely a pipe dream for me. True emotional maturity comes from the process of spiritual self-actualization. Guided meditation is still an essential tool for me to learn to make peace with the Void and emptiness. Without making peace with your cravings, you cannot hope to contain or surpass them in the long run. Guided meditation is also my primary weapon against relapse outside of my creative side. It centers me in the present instead of depression about the past or anxiety about the future. The future remains solely influenced by current actions, so fear about the future is a drain of your soul's potential abundance. As for the past, you can never change what has been and gone no matter how much you want to, so meditating on what cannot become undone does little good for you to grow emotionally. Through the guided meditation, emotional maturity and experience are a steadfast presence, present without past or future as any remote concerns. Guided meditation is difficult, for it requires focus and the willingness to do nothing to become sharper than attuning yourself to the present. We live in a world that thrives on consumption, greed, and falling prey to our sins and frailties, so that institutions can exploit us for cold hard cash. Practices such as meditation accomplish similar mental breakthroughs as psychedelics when mastered because they allow you to see through the consumerist lies that modern culture has fed you for decades. While maintaining sobriety is my goal on a daily basis, I will love marijuana until my dying breath. It can enhance creativity, make music sound incredible, and is fun the way alcohol is without the physical overdose potential or any debilitating withdrawal symptoms. But Marijuana did more damage to my life than any other drug by a long shot. It made me comfortable, even eventually, accepting of being a deceptive, backstabbing liar to people I love because the drug was so important to me. I was willing to bypass moral boundaries that I had spent years developing in favor of the high. It made me happy with existing at 25% of my true potential and capabilities without any conscious awareness of my severely reduced motivation. Because I never realized how comfortable I had become while remaining stoned, rather than facing the uncomfortable reality I had constructed through my self-deceptive marijuana fog. Here is some life advice. Thoughts that occur in a mindset lacking balance and self-actualization are self-destructive and primarily a waste of both time and soul. Stop doing it! One of the biggest reasons Cannabis reduced my motivation was because it made me critically overthink everything with an acute sensitivity, which made taking action much more intangible. Cannabis doesn't do this to everyone, as there are successful people such as Seth Rogen, Joe Rogan, Barack Obama and Willie Nelson, but for most addicts and me it becomes the goal in and of itself, not an augment or an asset to those goals.

When I started smoking weed the first two years and had a low tolerance, the drug often forced me to confront myself and helped me to experience additional dimensions of my reality. It felt like medicine to soothe the soul and enliven the senses! I would then apply those truths while remaining sober on weekdays, every week with a clear head. Given honest self-reflection, that was the only time that marijuana was a healthy activity for me in any fashion.

The other eight years of marijuana smoking were always about numbing out my emotions, both positive and negative and escaping both reality and eventually, my responsibilities. It was also my favorite anesthetic for numbing out fear of failure and avoiding social interactions because of the same fears of failure and rejection. The longer I smoked weed and the more weed I smoked, the more paranoid, lazy, and antisocial I became with every hit. Still, I did not give a fuck, because in my deluded reefer-soaked brain, it was healing my traumas by taking away all the intense emotions—good and bad. It was authentic because I was a zombie with no feelings or motivation by the end of my Cannabis habit. I did not care about anyone or anything at all, especially myself. I hated myself for being so weak and unwilling to look at my self-destructive behaviors. So, I self-medicated with marijuana and other drugs because I could then easily hide from these problems. By the end, I was an addict by necessity, to numb myself to the negative consequences of being mentally addicted and smoking and using for the sake of using. By the end, I wasn't using these substances to enhance or develop any activities or life goals, which was the exact opposite reason why I became attracted to psychoactive drugs originally. I abused all other substances from 2019 to early 2020 to numb myself to the consequences of both physical and psychological addiction.

———————●———————

Marijuana did more damage to me, not because of the drug itself, but because of my ingrained belief that it was *harmless*. It lulled me into this horrible false sense of security where everything was dangerously wrong, and eventually far from harmless. When I first quit, my writing ability was a quarter of what it was when I toked on weekends. When I smoked twice per week, I was constantly writing. At the beginning stage of my recovery, I found it hard to even think of ideas when smoking or not smoking. But when I was smoking, even if I did not come up with an idea, I felt too good to care about my wasted creativity, and that realization was horrible. If only I had just stuck to being a weekend warrior, or better yet never tried the drug at all. However, after that first year, I deliberately become a devout stoner. I could not imagine going a day, nay an hour, without THC in my soul. Moderation became an impossible fantasy at that very moment. Fuck moderation. I could not imagine a second without being stoned. My tolerance and potentially debilitating neurological symptoms from this *decision* was damned. When I first went to rehab, I did not give one fucking shit about anything for literally six horrible long dark years. I did a ton of hard drugs during that time but remained marijuana free against my will for three years. When I smoked pot again, the high was so intense and so beautiful that it sucked me in for six more years of misery. The battle cry, "**GOD, I CANNOT WAIT TO GET THE FUCK OUT OF HERE AND GET FADED AGAIN OFF THC AS QUICKLY AS POSSIBLE,!!!**"

What you do not have, you will never miss. Marijuana had twisted me up from the very inside out into someone I loathed and could not recognize anymore. No words can describe how much I will always both **TRULY LOVE** and **UTTERLY HATE** Cannabis for the rest of my life. The one thing I don't believe in regarding marijuana is the gateway theory. Other drugs have only **EVER** made me crave Pot 1,000,000 times more, not want to abandon it. It was my exit drug, never the gateway, until I tried opiates and then Cannabis alone was never enough to satisfy my cravings. I've wanted to do all mind-altering substances since middle school. Marijuana itself never encouraged me to try harder drugs.; that desire was already well in place. Cannabis was the only drug where I routinely underestimated its effect on my life, habits, and personality to the very end. I continuously denied the damage pot abuse was doing, because I needed it more than a crackhead needs crack. Cannabis is not evil, but it must be used responsibly, just like all mind-altering substances. They are not toys; they are powerful agents and landmines that can easily show you the gates of both Nirvana in artificial heaven and the very bottom of hellfire in the mere blink of an eye.

What I fear most is I will have years clean and sober and then start reminding myself of how *good* that high is. I believe this is true for all addicts in recovery. Relapse has the real potential to obliterate my soul from the inside out if I let drugs back into my lifestyle. I know that weed and opiates would take everything from me, but if I relapsed I would keep coming back for more and more like a brain-damaged prostitute. They are the only drugs that would make me lie through my teeth to maintain the highs. They would slowly destroy both my personality and character. I would be lying to myself and my loved ones to get just another glimpse into a world of synthetic escapism, which I have already visited too many damn times.

Marijuana was the only drug where I would sideline all of my responsibilities as I rationalized, I could do what I needed to while stoned. Initially, I could. When I had a low tolerance to weed during the first two years I performed normally because weed wasn't yet an everyday habit. In the end my responsibilities became impossible, as the necessity of my habit was paramount to all else. I was driven to keep the stoned escape going longer, but I always knew what came next and dreaded the comedown more and more as my tolerance increased. It took excessive amounts of the drug to get off properly by 2018. My tidal wave of grief and self-loathing increased the more marijuana I needed to smoke to get the same high that was easy to experience when I was a greenhorn. I knew that I was wasting my life away. I was becoming a shell of a human being, subverting all of my potential, all for a silly plant. After the first two years of blissful smoking, it was never worth it because I forgot to consume responsibly and only cared afterward about staying stoned at all costs. I wish my brain were ignorant of this delicious haze cloud of profoundly blissful, but stupidity-drenched ignorance.

It is medicinal, yet poisonous all at the same time. So remarkably subtle in its negatives, it steals years of your life and money and your soul without you even noticing. The other drugs broadside you, smashing you against the floor with a sledgehammer when you overstep your boundaries. At the same time, Cannabis slowly removes the layers of your life brick by brick until you suffocate with or without it.

I believe that it's vital to consume responsibly in all actions, drugs or anything else, or be prepared to watch the action consume you. When there is no going back, you will regret it for an eternity. **LESS IS ALWAYS MORE!!!** And if you cannot adhere to this principle, **STAY OFF THE TRAIN FOR DEAR LIFE!!!** Ignorance truly is bliss. Only now do I understand this philosophy which I once mocked as an *intellectual*. I now long for that ignorance and often salivate for it like Palov's slobbering dog. Artificial happiness gained by abusing pleasures of the flesh stimulates your dopamine receptors far beyond what they were programmed to release in the human body. Eventually, it destroys your serotonin, the chemical responsibly for happiness of the higher prefrontal cortex, whereas dopamine stimulates the receptors of the base brain (Avena et al, 2). Years after a series of traumatic middle school and high school events I had believed that I could not be creative without the aid of drugs and alcohol. I felt that my anxiety and restlessness were bad for creative purposes. Actually, these energies are the fuel for ANY creative ambition. Perpetually numbing them out is creative **POISON.**

Pain and challenges are creative fuel, while anxiety motivates human beings to better themselves in any endeavor. Pleasure and drugs are not evil or sin in and of themselves, but reliance on comfort (i.e., addiction to any behavior or routine) is the absolute sin; the destruction of ambition, creativity, and eventual success if anyone lets the desire for comfort as an end take over their lifestyle. It is not that smoking marijuana, drug use, or pleasurable behaviors are harmful or that these substances will ruin your life when used responsibly. It is when you make them a lifestyle or a coping mechanism for daily living that you become an addict (whether you admit it or deny it as I did), and your world's tunnels become small, isolated, and dark.

Pain, variety, and self-discipline go together. Success without them is utterly impossible. I see these three virtues as the cornerstone of all motivation and creative endeavors. Most people are undisciplined enough that they will live a lifestyle of denial, whether they admit it or not. The addict of any stripe is a special breed of this growth-stunting mentality. The addict has a particular fear and wants to avoid any changes, finding solace in routine, isolation, and comfort, often to their self-destruction if they cannot change themselves, or their coping mechanisms. Suppose we wish to eliminate or reduce addiction in society. In that case, we must teach people why self-restraint and discipline matter. We must offer education about tolerance, withdrawal symptoms, set (mindset), and setting (i.e., your mental and physical socio-economic environment).

It seems to me that people who depend on external stimulus to achieve internal happiness lack emotional maturity, and these people are the most likely to suffer from addiction. Most people blame the drugs themselves for drug addiction, but I was an addict, who at one point felt unable to be happy without external stimulus. I had to learn detachment from the self-defeating correlation between stimulus and happiness in order to change my ways. Suppose someone copes through escapism and is unwilling to accept responsibility for the reality of their actions or has undergone severe unresolved trauma or mental illness. In this case substance abuse is far more attractive and therefore, they are more susceptible to addictive behaviors than healthy, self-actualized individuals. It happened to me, and it took me years to realize this pattern and break the self-destructive cycle. Purpose is of vital importance to long-term recovery. Sobriety without purpose or engaging in behaviors to avoid figuring out one's purpose is no better than the disease of addiction itself. Many never make it back. They live and die miserably, because when they reach rock bottom, they cannot envision a life with or without drugs and alcohol. All addicts and alcoholics experience numerous bottoms, but rock bottom is an unrecoverable place, where most die or slip into insanity. I believe that it is nonsense to say that people need to hit rock bottom to recover from addiction. For most addicts, rock bottom means death via overdose or permanent insanity. If you still have something to live for, you haven't hit rock bottom and have a chance no matter how far down the scale you have gone. Most addictions stem from anger, fear, all emotions. There is an inability to sit alone in an empty room, accepting the void of death and the emptiness of being without external stimulus as a distraction. To transcend the need for an external motivation to gain or retain internal happiness is the key component to win the fight against addiction. Because all self-destructive habits come from an inability to be present, accept your current reality for what it is without fighting to alter it. Guided meditation is also an essential recovery tool, even more than personal fitness. When guided meditation is mastered, it gives people the ability to fully accept the present moment without alteration, a feat few humans in our materialistic, cruel, competitive capitalism-soaked society will ever accomplish on their own.

A legend surrounding drugs is that narcotics provide such colossal happiness. According to legend, if you experiment with only one dose, it will be so pleasurable that you will get hooked for life. We have all known about the guinea pigs' investigations, where rodents were placed in confined spaces and offered switches to press. Each time they squeezed the switch, they got a portion of dope. Also, the rodents squeezed the switches constantly and remained high until they kicked the bucket. They would not stop to eat; they doped themselves to death. The researchers suggested that the narcotics were so enjoyable, so pleasurable, that the rodents could not control themselves from overdose or dependency. Later, it was determined that the study methodology was fundamentally flawed. The scientists who led these experiments were not cheating. They were straightforward men attempting to get empirically and verifiable outcomes. These researchers neglected to take an important factor into consideration. They overlooked the nature of rodents. Rodents, like human beings are entirely extroverted creatures. They cannot stand being held in isolation; the way rodents were in these trials. For rodents as it would be for people, prolonged isolation is an unadulterated torment. Other researchers attempted another experiment with the same rats who survived the previous study—they created a Rat Park. They fenced a grassy oasis with bushes and trees, toys, saucer wheels, providing a great deal of room for the rats that they placed inside. At that point, they gave the rodents two dishes of water that they could drink. One contained morphine, and the other did not. They could drink all they needed whenever they chose too. The rats in this study rarely drank from the morphine bowls (Orange, 1).

The researchers even had a go at bribing the rodents to get them to drink morphine by dosing the opiated arrangement with sugar. It ought to have worked because rodents love sugar, yet it did not. The rodents would seldom drink it. It seemed that the rodents hardly ever wanted to get loaded on morphine when they had options and freedom. So, for reasons unknown, when in prolonged isolation, rodents will remain high and whacked out constantly. However, they do not care for being dopey when they are in an open-ended domain, spending time with their companions. Rodents, like humans, are self-motivated. The exception is when they are locked up in steel cages confined in a research center. Incidentally, most people have a similar mindset.

It is an old stereotype that the least fortunate individuals who live in disadvantaged neighborhoods and those who live on the streets are alcoholics and/or stoned throughout the day. Unfortunately, that is probably a reality. People who have nothing to lose have no incentive to get healthy. Many people, in better situations with better opportunities, would truly prefer not to get loaded constantly or avoids getting high at all. Think about two psychological tests like this yourself. In situation one, there is a person who is locked in jail, perhaps perpetually. This convict does not know if he will make parole or if he will ever see the light of day again. There is a lot of liquor and dope accessible. In Hari's "Chasing the Scream, he documented that *The War on Drugs* cannot keep narcotics out of maximum-security prisons (Hari, 2015). Does the convict drink and use? It's highly likely when the fatigue and protracted isolation invade his mind. Does he use enough to black out? Most likely.

In the second scenario, a person earns a well-deserved job promotion and is partying in an extravagant hotel suite with exotic Swedish escorts. Once more, the full inventory of liquor and mind-altering drugs is easily accessible. Does he use it? Possibly. Perhaps a bit. Does he remain high habitually? Profoundly unlikely, because it is difficult to charm those excellent ladies when you are strung out or too loaded. We can create another example of this psychological test. However, this time, make situation one a hopeless old apartment building in an awful part of town, where everyone shouts at one another and loathes one another, and where fights are constant. They steal from one another, and no one has any expectation that things in this neighborhood will ever achieve socio-economic improvement. Situation two is a beautiful bungalow on five acres of land of lush land at the edge of town, where the neighbors are decent, genial and hard-working folks for the most part, and everyone has steady employment. Need I even proceed? Presently we live in a psychological Rat Park, similar to a physical Rat Park. We carry our psychological condition around with us inside our own heads. What is more, I think that many of our responses to medications, or desires for drugs, are because of that perspective. (This is a major piece of the response to that old inquiry of "How does it occur here? What's causing the children to get stoned in our great white picket fence neighborhoods?") We are also live-in sociocultural domain, where external stimuli fundamentally impacts our individual, internal biochemistry and the subsequent decisions, promoted through sociocultural conditioning, from which we deduce right and wrong.

Our desires for drugs are due to that natural chemistry. Is everyone high? No. Is it true that one is in ten individuals are substantial dopers? No. One out of every hundred? Possibly. Perhaps a few, if you include the pill poppers, the stoners and the drunkards, and the cokeheads, and the speed-freaks, and the doctor shoppers, and so on. We have many individuals who feel awful. They feel so terrible that they need to get loaded or high just to feel OK. Be that as it may, they are a small minority. Furthermore, how hard is it to get drugs or liquor or pills? Pathetically simple. Prohibition is a failure. Everyone who wants to do drugs is, as of now, doing them already. Prohibition has failed and will forever remain a failure. It is a waste of both taxpayer dollars and human resources. Moreover, how terrible is it? We can inventory an exceptionally extensive rundown of social ills brought about by drugs alcohol. There are truly a ton of awful catastrophes. Yet, society, in some way or another, endures in any case. We are still here. Also, the greater parts of us have lives that are rich and full, despite adversities. Furthermore, in my opinion, many of the drug issues we endure in society exist because drugs are misguidedly illegal; these public policies and the public opinion of drug use in general is beginning to shift in alignment with my perspective. Addicts burglarize our homes because they need cash to purchase dope. Young people turn toward prostitution to earn cash so that they can purchase drugs. They would not do that if they could purchase drugs of pure quality, legally, and cheaper than on the black market. As well, we would not have Uzi-toting sellers shooting it out in the back alleys if there was anything but an enormous profit in it.

If the law worked, drugs would be harder to acquire, not easier than ever before. There are many individuals who shout, "We can't legalize drugs. We need to spare those poor addicts from themselves." Baloney. To those individuals I say, stop being a wolf in sheep's clothing. You could not care less about those addicts. In your eyes, they aren't human beings, but only disgusting, malodorous parasites who will steal all that you have when your back is turned. You do not want them near your home. What is more, you will not be sobbing late into the night if a junkie overdoses. You never went downtown to give a blanket to some sordid shivering withdrawing junkie on a cold winter night. I was there. I know the homeless on Venice Beach's streets, and I did not see you there. I did see a couple of kind-hearted spirits who did just that. Much obliged to them. What is more, the odd thing is that those soft-hearted individuals who were giving out the blankets were the least hypocritical individuals around. They didn't tell the addicts what to do with their lives or what to put into their bodies. They just helped them.

The ignorant and selfish individuals will do nothing for the addicts. Instead, they proclaim that we need to save junkies from their drug addiction by placing them in jails. The problem here is that drugs are as readily available in jails and maximum-security prison facilities, as they are on the streets. It is far from enough to have DARE in our schools. We need serious harm reduction classes required by federal law that talk about the importance of set and setting, tolerance, withdrawals, and safety precautions. This does not just go for drugs and alcohol, but any addiction (which can be anything someone enjoys enough to neglect or damage other balances in their life or relationships, no matter how healthy or condoned they may be a societal basis). When you tell people to stay away from the forbidden fruit, you need to assume that at least 1% will take a bite no matter their character. Trauma, segregation, and mental illness never discriminate based on a person's kindness or selflessness or upbringing. When the root of suffering is powerful traumatic experiences or issues of mental health, which distort a person's view of the world, they will desire any semblance of relief or escape and be willing to cross moral lines.

———————⬤———————

It is clear to me that *The War on Drugs* is immoral and must end with federal and state legalization and regulation. Rather than throwing addicts into cages, the profits from the legal, billion-dollar drug industry could be invested into updating rehabilitation centers for the 21st century. By scapegoating one category (drugs) as the cause of addiction itself, we are able to easily deny and disregard all other self-destructive non-drug addictions, which are currently affecting our culture and society adversely and unabated. I don't believe that anyone, from a grade-level student to a venerated government politician, can preach only one biased viewpoint of any issue, no matter how controversial and claim it as remotely educational. If *Just Say No* worked, the *Opiate Epidemic* would never have happened, and Purdue Pharma wouldn't be one of the richest corporations in the world—but millions of Americans became addicted to opiates. Despite getting millions of people addicted to OxyCodone, Purdue is being allowed to pay off court settlements with more opiate sales (Hoffman, 1-2). Adults misguidedly rationalize lying to children about controversial or dangerous subjects to protect them from vices but lying to dissuade people's attraction to vices never works, and this tactic has backfired hideously.

There is no reward without risk. Pleasure does not exist without pain, the yin-yang duality of natural law. We do not need a War on Drugs anymore, or ever again. We need a War on Addiction itself, or we will not get anywhere! There are numerous individuals who shout, "We can't sanction drug use. We can't have those addicts lying around, feeling great constantly." Baloney. Stop being a Puritan. It is of no concern to these people whether addicts feel better or worse. They ruthlessly support policies that ensure nothing changes for addicts. It will not destroy or improve their day unless a policy change affects their bottom line. Morality has nothing to do with the motivations behind the drug war. It's purely about profit and exploitation of racial divides and the socioeconomic underclasses. Like the Eagles' melody says, *Get Over It*. A few addicts are killing themselves. What of it? Get over It. A few addicts are feeling incredible euphoria from their addictions. What of it? Get Over It. Get Over It. It has nothing to do with you or your bliss. Parents discuss their youngsters and how they need to spare their kids from the dangers of liquor and drugs. Yet they support policies that make drugs more dangerous, not less. Their focus is on incarceration, prohibition, and shame, which are tools that enliven the very disease they proclaim to fight. Instead, the profits from incarceration need to get funneled into updating rehabilitation to include modernized mental health and trauma work, in addition to removing the criminal elements of the drug trade that make accessibility so easy.

———————●———————

The prohibitionists argue that hard drugs are killing fewer people because they are illegal, but the law has failed to keep these drugs out of people's hands from the very start. It has nothing to do with the law and everything to do with the Rat Park experiment, which society shamefully ignored for far too long. The people who feel trapped in an isolated cage, both in mindset and economic options, are infinitely more likely to become addicts than those with economic opportunity and a healthy social circle. The people who feel they have nothing to lose through self-destructive behaviors have no reason to stop or change. That is why letting addicts hit bottom is often a death sentence.

Most rehabilitation centers do not treat addiction properly because they focus on alcohol and drugs as the only problem without dealing with the underlying potential depression, traumas, mindset, or pain that leads patients to abuse substances or toward compulsive behaviors in the first place. It is not enough to change people's minds about Prohibition's failure; it is up to stable societies to promote harm reduction policies that challenge a misguided societal view of drugs, mental illness, and addiction. Christopher Hobson cited the 1961 Single Convention on Narcotic Drugs as a failure. The convention used the word evil to describe narcotic habituation, therefore, bypassing the more significant social and mental health causes that drove individuals towards addictive excesses (Hobson, 526). Drugs are chemicals neither living nor dead. They are neither evil nor benign. When you make drugs a lifestyle then the problems begin; the people who consumed or abhorred their consumption invented labels for these chemicals in our greater society. According to the United Nations Office for Drug

Control, 90% of people who use psychoactive drugs do not become addicted (Hari, 147). Further supporting research from Professor Craig Reinarman endorses the concept of natural recovery (Reinarman, 440).

This process is not unusual. According to John Marks's research, addicts stop or moderate drug use whether they receive treatment or not, if *The War on Drugs* does not destroy their chances at a better life first. This is called natural remission. The average time this takes is approximately ten years, with heavier use concentrated in addicts aged 25 to 39, after which habituation stabilizes (Hari, 212). Another study done by Reinarman discovered that many heroin addicts invent custom detoxes to get off opiates without needing rehabilitation (Reinarman, 440). On the other hand, Waldorf and Biernacki's research confirmed addicts' patterns of controlled use of narcotics that were thought to remain inherently addictive and impossible for the user to take in a controlled fashion (known as chipping) (Reinarman, 440). Therefore, the complex set of behaviors referred to as *drug abuse* is non-linear. Drug taking is based on adaptive responses that operate according to the norms of modern society's subculture, countercultural norms, and drug culture (Reinarman, 440). Further supporting research from the Journal of Ethnicity in Substance Abuse confirms that drug use (not drug addiction) becomes connected to the social fabric of a broad demographic of cultures, not just addicts (Myers & Stolberg, 68-69). Most United States citizens are unaware of the extent that the drug culture influences upon modern society. In Southern European societies, they consider alcohol a healthy part of every meal. The Swazi warriors of South Africa smoked Cannabis to help subdue hunger during long marches (Myers & Stolberg, 68-69). Steve Jobs once described taking LSD and smoking marijuana as two of the single most important actions he undertook in his young life, which enabled him to think differently and later, led to the creation of the Macintosh computer and mainstreamed Apple as a company (Isaacson, 41). Carl Sagan extolled Cannabis and its potential for consciousness expansion (Hendricks, 4). In Sagan's own words: "The illegality of cannabis is outrageous, an impediment to full utilization of a drug which helps produce the serenity and insight, sensitivity and fellowship so desperately needed in this increasingly mad and dangerous world" (Hendricks, 4). However, I have little doubt that Sagan was a temperate, rare Cannabis consumer given his consistent genius and creative output. Anthropologist Barbara G. Meyerhof's ethnographic study of Huichol Indians showed how their use of the hallucinogen peyote remained interwoven into ritualistic symbols of personal and social redemption (Myers & Stolberg, 68-69).

It's important to note that the chemical known as Ibogaine has become an underground breakthrough in the treatment of opiate addiction. Many users reported successful detoxes without opioid withdrawal symptoms. At the same time, the Ibogaine forced them through a psychedelic trip specifically to confront old addictive thinking patterns. While on this drug, the patient replaced old thought patterns with stronger and healthier mindsets. The Ibogaine recovery rate for drug addicts is 70% to 80% when followed by a rehabilitation program. This is an unheard-of statistic in addiction treatment. However, Ibogaine must be administered by knowledgeable professionals, who are experienced at determining dosage based on both the patient's weight and drug intake history. Several deaths have been attributed to improper clinical doses (American Addiction Center, 3). This moment-of-clarity experience is what both the psychedelics Salvia and Psilocybin accomplished for me long-term with the added benefit of trauma treatment. With these I realized that I would never survive to become the man I had the potential to become if I continued my addiction. Without a commitment to sobriety, self-control, or temperance, I will fall by the wayside through no one's fault but my own, just as thousands of addicts and alcoholics experience daily.

The War on Drugs blatantly ignores these statistics and focuses on the wrong approach. Ten percent of problem users are put forward as representing as the entire picture of drugs, users and addiction. Prohibitionists and advocates of the drug war tirelessly extinguish freedom, due process, liberty, compassion, and proper medical and mental healthcare initiatives for the sake of perpetuating tired and false stigmas while supporting private prison profiteering. Not only has *The War on Drugs* not reduced the supply of illegal narcotics, but it has also easily enabled criminals to become wealthy while capitalizing on acts of violent, sadistic brutality to control the supply of illegal drugs. According to Associate Professor Amy C. Carpenter from the University of San Diego, since 2006, Mexico and Central America have experienced unprecedented increases in savage violence because of the drug war (Hari, 116). Under socioeconomic and cultural control by cartel gangs, Mexican citizens have been desensitized to civilian, criminal executions which are the result of daily warfare. They openly witness regional Zeta gang members vying for control over the flow of narcotics, particularly cocaine and opiates (Hari, 116). The current Mexican political strategy is still based on boosting militarization, which ignores high-level government corruption that no one has the desire to resist, while ignoring a weak authoritarian substructure incapable of stopping these brutal injustices (Carpenter, 139).

Due to prohibition, which makes drugs a more valuable commodity without the law of taxation, sadistic acts of violence are rewarded by allowing drug dealers to control both the narcotics trade and the flow of customers. For a peddler of hard narcotics, the rule is always to stay strapped, because other drug traffickers wish to kill the competition to gain more illegal drugs and clients. Therefore, Rodrigo Duterte's foolish crusade in the Philippines to execute dealers and even drug users in an act of mass genocide solved zero problems related to addiction, while decimating the poor communities; his acts fueled an already deadly industry built on death and internal corruption. Naturally, these laws didn't apply to Duterte, despite his admission of being an abusive fentanyl user (Coonan, 1). Drug dealers do not fear death threats from politicians or government officials, because they are accustomed to other drug dealers wanting to kill them and steal their customers and dope anyway. When you steal a television out of a Best Buy, you sell it at a discount price because in this case, the market value is reduced as the television is now a used legal product. But if a drug dealer steals another dealer's stash of cocaine and heroin worth $1000, they get to sell the cocaine and heroin for $1000 or cut the drugs with adulterants to jack up the price. There is no discount on popular illicit drugs! Under prohibition, your child needs no identification to get their hands on dangerous narcotics. They fork over the cash, and the drugs are immediately in their hands.

CHAPTER 15

THE END OF THE WAR ON DRUGS MUST BEGIN WITH THE WAR ON ADDICTION ITSELF!

IF A PSYCHOACTIVE CHEMICAL IS UNREGULATED ON THE LOCAL BLACK market, no safe dose can be administered. In the legal prescription drug market, the customer has the right to product and purity information before they consume the medication. The goal of drug prohibition was to remove easy access to mind-altering compounds and to make the public safer. I have seen firsthand how this approach has failed entirely. The result has created a booming underground black market where poor addicts commit crimes to pay exorbitant prices for illegal narcotics, while wealthy users do not have to commit crimes to feed their habit (Machan, 86). History does not paint prohibition in a favorable light. When alcohol was placed under a ban, during Prohibition in the 1920s, crime rates skyrocketed; excessive drinking continued unabated, as whiskey and gin became more toxic to consume in bootleg form. Al Capone ruled the underworld with an iron fist until Prohibition was repealed in 1933 (Machan, 86). If the law legalized the mere possession of drugs, dispensaries and institutions would gain the ability to test all psychoactive compounds correctly. Legalization would enable manufacturers and government agencies to regulate potency and provide each exact dose with a numerical representation, so that users knew the correct dosage and could avoid an overdose. Using legal marijuana as a framework, it appears that this regulation has not successfully been implemented, and the black-market for illegal drugs still thrives. The only way to severely reduce the power of the black-market trade is to reduce the heavy taxes applied to legalized marijuana (Halperin, 2). I have also observed that if the consumer were able to get marijuana from legal dispensaries, where the weed is consistently more potent than black- market weed, the power of criminal trades would be greatly reduced.

The key to controlling one's habits, or changing one's habits, is a lifelong process for people whether they struggle with addictive behaviors or are non-addicted individuals. Recovery and change always begin with self-acceptance or end with inevitable suicide and self-destruction. We are creatures of habit. We have a constant need to connect with others and to feel validated from within ourselves. But, if people think that the only way, they can belong is through the validation of others around them, they will lose their way. Steve Jobs brilliantly articulated this philosophy in his famous Stanford graduation speech. "Your time is limited, so don't waste it living someone else's life. Don't be trapped by dogma—which is living with the results of other people's thinking. Don't let the noise of other's opinions drown out your own inner voice. And most important, have the courage to follow your heart and intuition" (Satara,4). If you lose the ability to love yourself, you have no capacity to love others. Without self-love, you will always find nothing but empty vessels of pain, raw as the sting of bitter winds over a quiet beach in the dark of the night.

My advice to all recovering addicts would be that with your life, fight the enemy of overthinking more than anything else to triumph over the roadblocks. I have found that when I am idle too long and stuck in my head, self-destructive darkness has its best crack at my psyche. You need to stop thinking in a generalized goal-oriented way. I tried this, and it failed miserably. Remember, goals are for people with no awareness of the steps needed to get there. Systems are for winners. Systems are about living ten to thirty seconds at a time and breaking down your dreams into the smallest tasks daily, so that the small choices you achieve daily will create bigger successes.

In my experience, if you adopt the AA attitude of powerlessness over your life, then your behavior will always match this belief. When you look inside yourself without judgements and accept the exact person who in front of you, warts, sins, and all, this is when healing can begin. To love yourself despite your flaws provides the fuel to stop digging your own grave and come up for air. Without compassion, flexibility, rationality, or sensible drug policy, *The War on Drugs* will only claim more and more lives rather than help save these lives from destruction. It is time for *The War on Drugs* to meet its well-deserved end. There is one supreme irony in that America refuses to acknowledge this, which we must address given our societal issues with addiction. It is the fact that we live in a culture whose economy thrives on addictive, impulsive behaviors while lying to ourselves about the desire to eliminate dependence; our economy runs and operates through dependencies.

Added to this, technology has increased modern convenience at the cost of meaningful human interactions. So, we are increasingly fragmented, isolated, and alone, therefore increasingly addicted to filling the holes because we are lacking healthy social interaction. Our economy runs on human shortcomings, not self-love, communal love, or self-empowerment. We are constantly bombarded with commercials that point out our weaknesses and how investing in material goods will satisfy the holes within our hearts when in reality only genuine human connections can fill that hole. Our increasing reliance on social media and technology has led to a more enabled and isolated culture where we make our friends through screens and smartphones instead of gaining conversational skills or taking chances out in reality! If anyone thinks the American government wants anything to change, history certainly disproves this assumption! Our mental healthcare system is not about self-empowerment or health. It is about using tough love and one-size-fits-all approaches that keep mentally ill people stuck in a revolving door of self-destructive treatment plans. These treatments heavily emphasize the self's core weaknesses and the need for unhealthy dependency on others or other things to produce inner peace, which is impossible to achieve.

If anyone also believes that America wants to eliminate addictive behaviors in people, you are remarkably deluding yourself! Our economy runs on impulsivity and feeding people a constant bombardment of insecurity to enforce materialistic and reckless actions to fill holes within themselves. The more independent and self-actualized people become—interdependent, self-disciplined individuals who can think for themselves and question authority to serve the needs of both themselves and others—the less money our government stands to siphon from the uneducated masses. Hence, power and control through fear and social coercion are imperative tools of capitalist imperialism. To create a society based on love, self-actualization, and free of addictive tendencies, our communities must be organized to displace greed and competitiveness over cooperation. Sadly, I cannot imagine that this will ever happen easily, as we are all fueled by greed in an increasingly isolated, fragmented, and addicted world. Unfortunately, we have turned to materialism, chemicals, and consumerism to fill the void because we are increasingly alone, and therefore increasingly addicted. Perhaps if we evolved to become a society that values organic connection over having more power than another, our economy would disintegrate; an outcome the American government dreads most but lies about desiring. Self-actualized, non-addicted people cannot be controlled by multimedia propaganda. Therefore, these people are a threat to the current American culture at the subconscious level. It would appear that our educational system is designed to make people just intelligent enough, but not clever enough to become critical thinkers, who can clearly recognize the prison of systematic, sociocultural indoctrination within which they are bred.

It appears our economy runs on human insecurity and impulsivity, yet constantly yammers on about a societal emphasis on health and wellness. The creators of the cartoon series South Park, Matt Stone and Trey Parker ("I'm A Little Bit Country"), got it right. America has become a nation whose philosophy promotes one lifestyle and directly profits from the exact opposite behaviors, saying one thing and doing another. We have become a nation of hypocrites because we encourage state and federal policies but legislate the opposite results. After all, governments profit from the system staying exactly the way it is. They will fight to the bitter end to ensure that this system remains the same because for the system to become healthy would mean the end of their own economic benefits! Thousands of mentally ill people are dying from this broken mental healthcare hierarchy that benefits the few at the expense of millions of families. When someone who struggles day-by-day to stay sober goes through *rehabilitation*, they are taught to admit that they are powerlessness over their addictions and ability to recover. This delusion is a deadly, self-fulfilling prophecy for people with serious mental illnesses and trauma, exacerbating both their maladaptive behavior and addictions. These techniques are employed purposefully because addiction and mental illness counselors would never make a six-figure annual income by empowering people to heal themselves. Thus, our recovery subculture remains cruelly designed as a revolving door to perpetuate the very condition it claims to treat, a blatant and deadly lie. If this corrupt societal substructure is not destroyed, addiction will only consume future generations at deeper levels, never to wither away as it should.

I have learned that the most effective way to take charge of your life is to uproot childhood trauma through the Buddhist principle of detachment (Brown, 2; Levine). When we remain attached to our emotions The attachment to our emotions allows them to control us and mold us in ways that are fundamentally self-depreciating and deceptive. The attachment to material desires blinds us to the self-care necessary to build wealth, let alone sustain it. Attachment to our past trauma robs us of the present mindfulness necessary to make non-addictive choices that benefit not only ourselves, but the communities around us. Through a combination of guided meditation, systematic incremental living and learning how to separate our emotions from our behaviors, we can evolve from reactivity to neutrality. Just as someone who smokes a joint doesn't become an addict in one day, learning emotional regulation and neutrality is a piecemeal practice that is tackled in small incremental self-observations and adjustments throughout that person's lifetime going forward. This is a crucial blueprint for healing and personal growth. We can change from our past beliefs into the indestructible forces of nature we have always dreamed of becoming. In taking care of your mental health, the realization that one size doesn't fit all is elemental for recovery. If you limit your rehabilitation options according to popular consensus, you will never unearth the root cause of your demons and be able to overcome them. Take great care in finding a mental health partner who will support your dreams and not shame you for them. Recovery is one day at a time, sometimes ten to thirty seconds at a time. If you relapse, remember that the more you kick yourself down for doing so, the deeper down the rabbit hole you will tumble!

FAVORITE QUOTES & CATCHPHRASES

"Talk less, listen more."

"The root of most maladaptive behaviors comes from unresolved trauma, particularly childhood trauma. It doesn't matter how much you chastise a bad behavior, without uncovering and healing the root trauma that makes a mentally ill patient unable to cope with reality, they will continue recidivist coping mechanisms no matter what the consequences."

"Your time is limited, so don't waste it living someone else's life. Don't be trapped by dogma—which is living with the results of other people's thinking. Don't let the noise of other's opinions drown out your own inner voice. And most important, have the courage to follow your heart and intuition" (Satara,4).

"Time is the greatest and most valuable currency available in all of life, because it can never be replenished by any amount of money you spend. Money comes back, time never will. The wealthy desire time more than they desire money, and that is why they are rich because they spend money to get time, not to get more money. Once your time comes to die, the time you squandered, the opportunities you believed were a waste of *time*, will haunt your final hours to the grave."

"Detachment Over Attachment. Neutrality Over Reactivity."

"Emotions are terrible servants and cruel masters. They will betray you to satisfy any impulse no matter how self-sabotaging the results."

"The wisest sober man or woman can become as selfish, sinful, and obnoxious as a drunkard with enough power and success to blind them." In the words of Bill Gates: "Success is a menace! It fools smart people into thinking they cannot lose."

"The use of drugs and alcohol are only servants to fully self-actualized human beings, and pure poison to all the rest. Before drinking or using consistently note your set and setting. Are you happy with your life? Do you have a fully defined sense of purpose and realized potential? Without these crucial elements, addiction and self-destruction is fated inevitability for both the strong and the weak-willed."

"Thinking is heavily destructive, a total waste of both time and soul. Quit doing that bullshit!" In the words of Andre 3000: "When you think too much, you're removing what's moving!"

"Money is not the root of all evil. The addiction to power is."

"Prayer is 95% of the time begging God to do your work for you because you're too entitled, weak, or lazy to get up off your ass and hustle hard to make your dreams come true. God does not answer them because the Lord only helps those who help themselves and nobody else."

"Comfort is a seductive prison that makes you feel amazing while robbing your dreams from you."

"The most uncomfortable, disturbed artists who are placed in the worst possible situations that will not kill them develop tolerance in being uncomfortable to become successful. They stay successful only by seeking discomfort and greater challenges and prosperity can threaten their very extinction."

"Denial and dishonesty are the best of friends to the purest of souls when the truth is too disgusting or dystopian to accept or comprehend."

"Vengeance and revenge are the seductive pitfalls to self-destruction and ruin."

"It is far better to be hated doing what you love in this life, then to be loved for doing what you loathe. A person without a purpose and willing to conform their dreams to the standards of others is better off deceased."

"There is no greater path to misery than to live by the dictates and limitations of other people's thinking."

"Failure is your blueprint to becoming greater than you already are. Success keeps you frozen in time."

"The only difference between mediocrity and success is the number of excuses versus the number of systems. Systems triumph over goals. Compartmental choices and the little details are 1,000% more important than the big picture will ever be."

"School is mostly a waste of time. You are being trained to be a minimum wage slave, not to become prosperous. The only lessons that matter is on the playground where you learn how to interact and relate to people outside of yourself and either gain humility within your ego or become consumed through materialism and egotism. Learn a trade and become a content creator. Learn how to help other people solve their problems and success is assured. The business world thrives on cooperation and interdependence, our education pushes independence and self-reliance, the opposite of what successful people in this world use naturally."

WORKS CITED

American Psychiatric Association. "Diagnostic and Statistical Manual of Mental Disorders, 5th ed. American Psychiatric Publishing, 2013.

Avena, N. M., Rada, P. and Hoebel, B. G. "Evidence for Sugar Addiction: Behavioral and Neurochemical Effects of Intermittent, Excessive Sugar Intake." *Neuroscience & Biobehavioral Reviews*, vol. 32, no. 1, Jan. 2008, pp. 20–39.

Brown, L. "The Real Meaning of Buddhist Detachment & Why Most of Us Get It Wrong." *Hack Spirit*, Brown Brothers Media, 7 May 2020, www.hackspirit.com/zen-master-explains-real-meaning-non-attachment-us-get-wrong/.

Burroughs, W., Ginsberg, A. and Pratsines, N. *Junky*. Apopira Publications, 1983.

Carpenter, A. "Changing Lenses: Conflict Analysis and Mexico's 'Drug War." *Latin America Politics & Society* volume 55, no. 3, Fall 2013, pp. 139-160.

Coonan, C. "Philippines Leader Duterte under Pressure over Own Drug Use," *The Irish Times*, Irish Times Trust, 14 Feb. 2017, www.irishtimes.com/news/world/asia-pacific/philippines-leader-duterte-under-pressure-over-own-drug-use-1.2975165.

Dettmer, P. "Why The War on Drugs Is a Huge Failure." *YouTube*, uploaded by Kurzgesagt-In a Nutshell, Mar 1 2016, https://www.youtube.com/watch?v=wJUXLqNHCaI.

Editorial Staff. "What Is the Success Rate for Ibogaine?" American Addiction Centers, 6 July 2021, www.americanaddictioncenters.org/meth-treatment/success-rate-for-ibogaine.

Halperin, A. "Can Legal Weed Ever Beat the Black Market?" *The Guardian*, Guardian Media Group, 18 Mar. 2019, www.theguardian.com/society/2019/mar/17/legal-weed-black-market-california-gavin-newsom.

Hari, J. *Chasing The Scream*. Bloomsbury, 2015.

Hendricks, S. "Carl Sagan on Why He Liked Smoking Marijuana," *Big Think*, Freethink Media, Inc., 16 Oct. 2018, bigthink.com/health/carl-Sagan-on-smoking-marijuana/.

Hoffman, J. "Purdue Pharma Is Dissolved and Sackler's Pay $4.5 Billion to Settle Opioid Claims." *The New York Times*, A.G. Sulzberger, 1 September 2021, www.nytimes.com/2021/09/01/health/purdue-sacklers-opioids-settlement.html.

Horsely, S. "Trip Of a Lifetime" *The Guardian*, Guardian Media Group, 19 June 2004, https://www.theguardian.com/theobserver/2004/jun/20/features.magazine67

Hobson, C. "Challenging 'Evil': Continuity and Change in the Drug Prohibition Regime." *International Politics,* vol. 51, no. 4, July 2014, pp.525-42.

Gilmore, Nicholas. "The World's First Bad Acid Trip." *The Saturday Evening Post*, Saturday Evening Post Society Curtis Publishing Company, 18 Apr. 2018, www.saturdayeveningpost.com/2018/04/worlds-first-bad-acid-trip/.

"I'm A Little Bit Country." *South Park*, created by Matt Stone and Trey Parker, season 7, episode 4, Comedy Central, 2003.

Isaacson, W. "Steve Jobs." *Simon & Schuster*, 2011.

Levine, N. "*Refuge Recovery: A Buddhist Path to Recovering from Addiction.*" HarperOne, 2014.

Machan, T.R. "Drug Prohibition Is Both Wrong and Unworkable.*" Think*, vol.11, no. 30, 21 December 2011 pp.85-92.

Naím, M. "Wasted: The American Prohibition on Thinking Smart in the Drug War.*" Foreign Policy*, no.172 May/June 2009, pp. 167-168.

Myers, P., and V. Stolberg. "Ethnographic Lessons on Substance Use and Substance Abusers." *Journal of Ethnicity in Substance Abuse,* vol. 2, no. 2, 2003, pp.67-88.

Van Olphen, J., Eliason, M., Freudenberg, N. and M. Barnes. "Nowhere to Go: How Stigma Limits the Options of Female Drug Users After Release from Jail." *Substance Abuse Treatment Prevention Policy*, 8 May 2009, pp.4-10, doi: 10.1186/1747-597X-4-10.

Orange, A. "The Effectiveness of the Twelve-Step Treatment." *Archive.org*, Orange Papers, 12 September 2015, web.achive.org/web/20161020131749/www.orange-papers.org/orange-effectivness.html.

Orange, A. "Rat Park and Other Children's Stories." *Archive.org*, 10 August 2015, web.archive. org/web/20160813143638/www.orange-papers.org/orange-ratpark.html.

Reinarman, C. "Beyond Deviance and Disease: Drug Users as Subjects at The Institute for Scientific Analysis," *Drugs: Education, Prevention & Policy,* vol. 19, no. 6 November 2012, pp.436-441.

Romance, L. "Live Nirvana Interview Archive," *Live Nirvana,* LiveNIRVANA, 10 August 1993, www.livenirvana.com/interviews/9308lr/index.php.

Satara, A. "Breaking down the Steve Jobs Quote That Helps Me Fulfill My Potential," *Medium*, Better Marketing, 19 Aug. 2019, bettermarketing.pub/this-steve-jobs-quote-is-my-mantra-its-brought-me-closer-to-living-my-best-life-90569d00c0d3.

So, J. "F. Scott Fitzgerald's 'on Booze': America's Drunkest Writer." *The Daily Beast*, The Newsweek Daily Beast LLC, 17 July 2011, www.thedailybeast.com/ f-scott-fitzgeralds-on-booze-americas-drunkest-writer.

Smith, S. "The Circularity of Trauma-Addiction-Trauma," *Core.ac.uk*, University Of South Africa, February 2016, core.ac.uk/reader/79170843.

Topalli, V. "Drug Dealers, Robbery and Retaliation: Vulnerability, Deterrence and the Contagion of Violence." *British Journal of Criminology*, vol. 42, no. 2, February 2015, pp. 337–351.

Twomey, S. "Phineas Gage: Neuroscience's Most Famous Patient." *Smithsonian Magazine*, January 2010, www.smithsonianmag.com/history/phineas-gage-neurosciences-most-famous-patient-11390067/.

Wilonsky, Robert. "Blood on the Tracks," *Phoenix New Times*, Voice Media Group, 12 Dec. 1996, www.phoenixnewtimes.com/music/blood-on-the-tracks-6423201.

Wilson, W. *Alcoholics Anonymous: The Story of How Many Thousands of Men and Women Have Recovered from Alcoholism*, 4th Ed. Alcoholics Anonymous World Services, 2001.

Printed in the United States
by Baker & Taylor Publisher Services